The House By The Lake

A Thriller

Hugh Mills

Samuel French–London
New York – Sydney – Toronto – Hollywood

Reproduced using
the
Halstan COPY BOOK System
Amersham, Bucks.

For
P.A.G.
with love

The House by the Lake

"The House by the Lake" was first presented by Peter Daubeny at the Duke of York's Theatre, London, on the 9th of May 1956, with the following cast:—

COLONEL FORBES	Frank Royde
STELLA	Jenny Laird
JANET	Flora Robson
BRENDA	Doreen Morton
MAURICE	Andrew Cruickshank
COLIN	Paul Lee
IRIS	Sylvia Coleridge
MR. HOWARD	Alan MacNaughtan
NURSE THOMSON	Annette Kerr

The play was directed by JOHN FERNALD.
Décor by FANNY TAYLOR.

CHARACTERS

in order of appearance:

COLONEL FORBES

STELLA

JANET

BRENDA

MAURICE

COLIN

IRIS

MR. HOWARD

NURSE THOMSON

The scene is the library of an old house in the country not far from London. The time is the present.

ACT ONE
A winter morning

ACT TWO
The same evening

ACT THREE

| SCENE ONE | .. | .. | .. | .. | The following afternoon |
| SCENE TWO | .. | .. | .. | .. | A few hours later |

No reference is intended, in this play, to any person, alive or dead.

The running time of this play, excluding intervals, is approximately two hours.

PRODUCTION NOTE

In repertory and amateur theatre varied choice in casting may not exist. Nevertheless, in producing *The House by the Lake* the cardinal principle of casting "against type" should be followed as closely as possible.

Janet's character, for example, has certain qualities of submissiveness and flexibility which could seem tiresome if the part were played by an actress in whose own personality these attributes were very noticeably present. If, on the other hand, Janet is played by a woman of marked strength of character, then the temperament of the actress will be found to blend with that of Janet and a three-dimensional and theatrically effective stage character will emerge.

Similarly Maurice could be an excessively unsympathetic creature if not played by an actor of considerable natural charm. Stella could become melodramatic if depicted by too hard a personality and Colin, in particular, could easily become "unbelievable" if "cast to type".

Mr. Howard, of course, is purposely written as a somewhat nebulous character. His true nature it is his business to conceal. He should be played by an actor in whom a pleasant but vague personality can be shown to hide a sharp apprehension of all that he sees going on about him.

As for Brenda, the maid, it is vitally important that she should be played, as she is written, perfectly "straight". The damage to the play's development and to its atmosphere will be enormous if Brenda is allowed to turn, even slightly, into the stock, comic servant.

As to the play itself let us take it act by act.

The main problem in the opening of Act One is to arouse the audience's interest in the information the author must give them during the first twenty minutes or so and which he does without the slightest attempt to titillate that interest by any particularly exciting theatrical device. A good pace must be obtained by the producer from the very beginning and it must be kept going. Colonel Forbes must not be allowed to become a bore and everything possible must be done to make him lovable and sympathetic. He is one of the few completely normal human beings in the play and the audience can be induced to have a fellow-feeling for him as soon as they begin to realize what a curious set of characters he has come among.

Stella has the hard task of putting over the essential facts, but her explanations will be made interesting if it is clear that she is under great emotional stress as a result of what she and her brother have decided to do that evening.

Janet's first appearance brings further explanations, but these will have an overtone of interest if Stella's attitude towards them is clearly marked and if it conveys a hint of the forces at work of which Janet knows nothing.

With Maurice's entrance the act begins to move with its own momentum and by the time he and his sister are alone together to discuss how the murder is to be carried out the play has got well under way.

Janet's decision not to go out to dinner is a striking theatrical effect and the reactions to it of Maurice and Stella should not be missed.

Colin's scene should be powerful but not overplayed and the producer should not overlook the comedy which colours the poignancy of Iris's duologue with Janet.

Comedy, too, as well as a feeling of mystery, pervades the short scene with Mr. Howard. Finally, in Janet's telephone conversation, which brings down the curtain of this act, it is, of course, important that the audience know that Janet *might,* after all, return home early.

Act Two. This is a fast-moving straightforward act, but there is one danger against which a producer must be on his guard: the succession of embarrassments suffered by Maurice and Stella, at being prevented from disposing of the body according to plan, must never relapse into bathos and become inappropriately comic. The different events—Brenda's return and her potterings in and out of the room, Janet's unexpectedly early reappearance—must be handled with variety. For example, not all of them should happen without warning and Janet's entrance, in particular, should be anticipated by both the conspirators and the audience by some such device as "voices off" or the sound of the opening front door. Failure to achieve this will bring unwanted laughter.

Another possible cause of unintentional comedy can be the cupboard—and the whole area round the cupboard—into which the body is placed. The audience must be allowed to forget this cupboard as much as possible once the body is inside. If it is too prominently placed in the scene or too brightly lit, or if too much emphasis is placed on it by the reactions of the conspirators, the tension of the audience will release itself in titters which will ruin the scene.

Finally, the conspirators must not allow their acting to become melodramatic: their attitude, both before and after the murder must be matter-of-fact and businesslike, cool and calculating.

Act Three. The matter-of-fact and businesslike approach should prevail in the first scene of this act in so far as the acting of the detective and also of Maurice and Stella is concerned. If this is done the growing distress of Janet will be thrown effectively into relief. Maurice's attitude towards his wife, when he realizes that the knowledge she possesses must mean her removal will be frightening in proportion to the lack of colour he puts into his performance. In the final scene again the belief in his power to hypnotize effectively will disappear if the slightest trace of melodrama is allowed to creep into his acting.

The hypnotism scene must be a *tour-de-force* for the actress who plays Janet. There can be no short cuts in learning how to play it, but this can be said, that it is a long scene, and that every possibility of variety of pitch, tempo and volume must be exploited in the playing. If variety is not achieved in sufficient degree the audience will become restless, longing, as they are, to see just exactly how Maurice is going to get her to shoot herself. Once the gun is in Janet's hands, the producer is in some difficulty for the play is virtually over, bar the eleventh hour twist which the audience is expecting. The counting must not be dragged—the detective should make his presence felt as Janet says sixteen or so (earlier is perfunctory, later loses tension), and, finally, he should enter the room somewhere about the late forties or early fifties (later than this would provoke the inevitable laugh).

Finally, it should be remembered that this play is not truly a "thriller", but a play of characterization and atmosphere. The producer must not take a rushed tempo; neither must he be slow. Above all he must see that his actors perform with sincerity, and with that sense of an inner world of thought and feeling of which the words they speak are but the audible, and partial, expression.

JOHN FERNALD

THE HOUSE BY THE LAKE

ACT ONE

The scene is the living-room of MAURICE HOLT'S *house in the country, not far from London.*
It is one of those large and rather gloomy Victorian houses and the room gives an impression of shabby grandeur. But it has a certain dignity and, many years ago, before it became so poverty-stricken, it must have been, in its dark, Gladstonian manner, very comfortable if somewhat grim.
Everything in it is old: old books on the shelves, one or two old pictures on the walls, one or two old leather chairs and a sofa.
There are very high french windows at the back leading into the garden. Outside there is snow and they are closed. The fireplace is in the right wall. Up right there is a door leading to the kitchen and other parts of the house and up left, another, leading to the hall. Near the latter, in a deep recess, there is a large, built-in cupboard with a solid, mahogany door exactly like the others. In this corner, up left, there is also a very small window.
When the curtain rises there is no one present. After a moment, however, COLONEL FORBES *appears outside the french windows; quite a fine old English gentleman: tall, thin, slightly aquiline—nothing soft or flabby about him. He suggests, in fact, considerable strength of character—a formidable old boy, but gentle.*
He is well wrapped up against the cold. He gently taps on the glass.

COL. FORBES. Anyone at home?
(He taps on the window again. Then he whistles, not very successfully, clears his throat and calls again.)
Hullo there!
*(*STELLA *enters from the kitchen. She is a plump, pale woman of about thirty-eight with short hair and a tight-fitting suit. No jewellery.)*
STELLA. Oh! Excuse me! One minute! I'll let you in!
(She opens the french windows, lets him in and then closes them again.)

COL. FORBES. Thank you. Good morning.

STELLA. Good morning, Colonel. I'm sorry about that.

COL. FORBES. Tried the front door. No reply.

STELLA. The maid's out. We were all upstairs.

COL. FORBES. Me own fault. Shouldn't call on people unexpectedly at eleven in the morning! But I had to pass the house. Thought I'd try me luck.

STELLA. Do sit down. Would you like some coffee?

COL. FORBES. Oh no . . . no, thanks. Never touch it. Heart, you know.

STELLA. I'm sorry. I *didn't* know.

COL. FORBES. No reason why you should.

STELLA. Is that recent?

COL. FORBES. Not very. Result of the Boat Race, 1920. Is your brother in, Miss Holt?

STELLA. He's in . . . yes. But . . . well, he's not up yet.

COL. FORBES. Ah. Ah. Then I'll call again.

STELLA. If you can wait a few minutes . . .

COL. FORBES. No, no . . . in a way it's rather a relief.

STELLA. A relief?

COL. FORBES. I'm a bit frightened of this . . . this . . . don't know what to call it really. This mission.

STELLA (*puzzled*). Mission?

COL. FORBES. Yes. Mission.

(COLONEL FORBES *stares about him, his mouth working nervously.*)

STELLA (*after a moment*). Well . . . of course I don't know what your mission is. But I can't imagine you being frightened of anyone, Colonel. Certainly not of my brother.

COL. FORBES (*letting out a deep breath*). Well . . . I am.

STELLA. Oh?

COL. FORBES. However . . . as he isn't up . . . it will have to be later.

STELLA. Well, you know he goes to bed very late. He sleeps very little. And anyway he hasn't very much to get up for . . . nowadays.

COL. FORBES. Well . . . perhaps he has, this morning. I'd like to think so.

STELLA. Would you care to tell *me* about it?

COL. FORBES. Well . . . at least you'll be able to advise me on the best approach.

STELLA. Do sit down, Colonel.

COL. FORBES (*doing so*). The thing is this. I think your brother . . . well, I think I might be able to help him.

STELLA. Yes?

COL. FORBES. About . . .

(*He hesitates.*)

STELLA. About his professional situation?

COL. FORBES. That's it.

STELLA. I can't imagine how.

COL. FORBES. Miss Holt, the new Chairman of the Medical Council is Sir Gordon White. A life-long friend of mine. We were at Eton together.

STELLA. And you think?

COL. FORBES. He should be able to help if anyone can . . .

STELLA. Do you mean with a view to . . .

COL. FORBES. I mean with a view to getting your brother back on the Medical Register. That's what I mean.

STELLA (*after a moment's pause*). It's extremely kind of you to have thought of this.

COL. FORBES. Not a bit. The only question is . . . would your brother . . . well, would he resent my, my, my . . . my interfering?

STELLA. I shall have to be quite frank about this, Colonel. I think he might. Please don't misunderstand me . . . it wouldn't be because it came from you . . . it would be the same whoever it was . . . Do please believe that. But the fact is my brother's very . . .

(*She stops.*)

COL. FORBES. Sensitive. Yes. I can see that.

STELLA. It's made a horrible mess of things.

COL. FORBES. Yes. We should have to be diplomatic. Clever. And I'm not very clever.

STELLA. Also . . .

COL. FORBES. Yes?

STELLA (*with an effort*). I think it's too late anyway.

COL. FORBES. Why?

STELLA. I don't think . . . even if he had the chance . . . that my brother would be likely to practise again . . . ever. At least not in England.

COL. FORBES. He's quite young. How old is he? Forty-five or fifty?

STELLA. It isn't a question of age, Colonel. The point is that for nearly ten years he's been . . . well, let's face it . . . in disgrace. What happened was exceedingly unjust. You don't imagine that living under such a cloud as that for so long has no effect.

COL. FORBES. Well, perhaps I'd better go and mind my own business.

STELLA. You haven't spoken to anyone, have you?

COL. FORBES. Haven't said a word. Talked it over with me wife. Came along here on her advice to talk it over with him. (*Rising.*) Seems to me that someone ought to do something. Stupid, this sort of thing.

STELLA. What made you think of this?

COL. FORBES. Well, I'll tell you. It's very interesting. I was talking to a fellow a week or two ago . . . member of my club . . . used to be a patient of your brother's. Don't know how we got on to the subject. Think I mentioned your brother was one of my neighbours down here. He talked about him for half an hour without stopping. Said he owed your brother everything he has. And he has plenty. Lovely wife . . . beautiful children . . . big position. Very happy normal type of fellow, you'd say. But apparently when your brother began to treat him he'd been for seven years in a mental home.

STELLA. Yes. I think I know whom you mean . . . though he wasn't the only one.

COL. FORBES. Seems a great pity that such a useful life as your brother's should be . . . well . . . thrown away. Thrown away.

STELLA. It's more than a great pity. It's a very great crime.

(*They turn as* JANET *enters up right.* JANET *is in the forties. She is beautiful, with dark hair and dark eyes. There is something strange about her, an air of sorrow and of resignation. She has been marked by some unhappiness. But she is graceful and slender, making her sister-in-law seem hefty in the contrast. She wears a soft, close-fitting Shetland sweater and a full skirt, both black. Her only ornament is a necklace of pearls.*)

JANET. Oh! Colonel Forbes! Good morning! I didn't know you were here.

COL. FORBES. Good morning, Mrs. Holt.

JANET. Do you want to see my husband?

COL. FORBES. Well, I *did*. But after talking to your sister-in-law I . . . well we . . . we, we think it might be a mistake.

JANET (*astonished*). A mistake?

STELLA. A very great friend of the Colonel's has become Chairman of the Medical Council. The Colonel was wondering whether to approach him.

JANET. About Maurice!

STELLA. Naturally.

COL. FORBES. Of course I was going to ask your husband first. But Miss Holt thinks I shouldn't do anything.

JANET. *Why* do you think he shouldn't?

STELLA. You know Maurice as well as I do, Janet. He would hate it.

JANET. I wonder if you're right about that.

STELLA. I'm sure I am.

JANET. In any case I don't think this is a thing that *we* should decide. I think the Colonel should talk to him. I think *Maurice* should decide.

STELLA. Well, of course, Janet dear. But you always do think Maurice should decide everything.

JANET (*with a smile*). You see, Colonel? I'm the perfectly dutiful, submissive wife. My sister-in-law laughs at me.

STELLA. However, I wasn't striking at Maurice's authority, Janet. I was only trying to protect him from something that I think might hurt him uselessly.

JANET. Still, it's a vitally important decision, Stella. Suppose we discovered years from now . . . when it was too late . . . that we'd done the wrong thing. (*To* COLONEL FORBES.) You think this might make it possible, really, for him to work again?

COL. FORBES. It *might*. I wouldn't say more than that.

JANET. Oh, my God, if only that were possible. Colonel Forbes, do you know *why* he was struck off the Medical Register?

COL. FORBES. Vaguely. Don't know the details, of course.

JANET. But there are no details. It was the simplest thing in the world.

STELLA. Janet, is there any need to go into all . . .

JANET. But of course there is! If he's going to talk to Maurice! (*To* COLONEL FORBES.) The whole disaster was caused by Maurice's and Stella's brother, Colin.

STELLA. Step-brother.

JANET. You haven't met him, I think.

COL. FORBES. No.

JANET. He's a financier. He lives in Grey Towers, that big house on the other side of the lake. You can see it from here. My husband was treating a patient . . . a woman . . . who was very rich. Her name was Mrs. Hoyle. A widow. He allowed her to invest some money in a company his step-brother was forming. And when I say "allowed her", I mean it. She was very insistent indeed. She was passionately devoted to investing money in private companies. Unfortunately this one went wrong. She lost two thousand pounds.

She was worth two *hundred* thousand. But she didn't take it quite so sportingly as she might have done. She brought a legal action against my husband and since he also had shares in this company it was easily made to look very bad. A psychiatrist who influences a patient to invest in . . . well, you can see.

STELLA. Incidentally, my brother had used hypnosis in treating her . . .

JANET. You can imagine the headlines—defenceless widow swindled by hypnotist, etc. Since then of course he's been disgraced and not allowed to work. Mrs. Hoyle died about a year ago. She left nearly two hundred thousand pounds for the foundation of homes for lost cats throughout Europe.

(BRENDA *enters from the hall.* BRENDA *is the maid. She is tall and thin and quite elderly. She has white hair and blue eyes and she speaks very gently and musically with a slight Irish accent. She is wearing a coat over her white apron.*)

BRENDA. I'm sorry to trouble you, ma'am, but a gentleman is at the front door.

JANET. Who is he, Brenda?

BRENDA. He says his name is Mr. Howard, ma'am.

JANET. Mr. Howard? I don't know a Mr. Howard. What does he want?

BRENDA. I don't rightly know, ma'am. He asked for Mr. Holt and when I said he wasn't up he asked could he speak to you.

JANET. I'll come and see. Brenda, would you go upstairs and ask Dr. Holt to come down? Colonel Forbes would like to see him.

BRENDA. Surely, ma'am.

JANET. Excuse me. One minute.

(JANET *goes out to hall and* BRENDA *up right.* COLONEL FORBES *takes his coat off.*)

STELLA. Well, there we are.

COL. FORBES (*smiling*). Mrs. Holt seems to know her own mind.

STELLA. Oh. On the contrary.

COL. FORBES (*puzzled*). I beg your pardon?

STELLA. A mind of her own is exactly what Janet does not have. You'll see. All she wanted, you know, was not to decide anything without asking him. That would have upset her very much.

COL. FORBES (*with a twinkle*). I must tell my wife about that!

STELLA. You find it abnormal. She was once very ill, you know.

COL. FORBES. She looks very well now. A little pale, perhaps.

STELLA. Oh, it wasn't a physical illness. Janet was what is called a manic depressive. She was unhappy to the point of suicide.

COL. FORBES (*horrified*). She tried to commit suicide? Mrs. Holt? But I . . . I can't believe that. She seems such a sweet person.

STELLA. Sweet people aren't barred from being unhappy.

COL. FORBES. You mean she really tried to kill herself? Or just threatened to?

STELLA. Well, she was found unconscious in a room full of gas with the door and the windows sealed on two different occasions. I suppose you wouldn't call that a mere threat?

COL. FORBES. Good God! I'd no idea. But . . . aren't you afraid she'll do it again?

STELLA. Not at all.

COL. FORBES. What, what . . . what was the cause of it?

STELLA. Well, a sort of profound anguish—melancholia. Due to all sorts of miseries when she was young.

COL. FORBES. And it's over?

STELLA. Yes. It's over.

COL. FORBES. Completely?

STELLA. Completely. She's cured.

 (MAURICE *enters up right. He is wearing pyjamas and a dressing gown. The moment one sees him one realizes that* STELLA *is right and that he will probably not work again. But in this derelict there are signs still of the splendid man he was.*)

MAURICE. Good morning, Colonel. Forgive me for receiving you like this. I didn't know which day you were coming.

COL. FORBES. You didn't know I was coming at all!

MAURICE. Oh yes. I expected you.

COL. FORBES. How's that? I sent no message.

MAURICE. As a matter of fact I expected you several days ago.

COL. FORBES (*astonished*). You did? But why?

MAURICE. I'll even tell you why you're here. Which will save you a lot of discomfort . . . since you're feeling so nervous about it. You've come to, well, to ask if you can do something to help me.

COL. FORBES (*after a moment*). Has my wife been talking to you?

MAURICE. No.

COL. FORBES. What else do you know?

MAURICE. Oh, nothing much. Except that you want to speak to Sir Gordon White about me.

COL. FORBES. Well I'm damned!

(*He looks at* STELLA, *bewildered.   Then at* MAURICE *again.*
MAURICE *stares at him gravely.*)

Well, you're quite right. But how do you do it?

MAURICE. I read about Gordon White's appointment a month or two
ago. And then . . . about a fortnight ago . . . you mentioned
that you knew him very well. I wondered why, but I didn't think
about it until Sunday night, when we were at your house and you
mentioned him again, dragging him into the conversation with great
difficulty. Your wife immediately left the room for no very good
reason. And then . . . though you made a desperate effort to do
so . . . you didn't manage to say anything. So of course I began to
wonder what was in your mind. That was all. It was very simple.

COL. FORBES. Was it?

MAURICE. Then—once I realized what was coming—I tried to decide
when to expect it. I said to myself "The colonel is a slow starter but
not a man to run away from anything. In a day or two he'll probably
come round here to beard the lion in its own den. And," I said to
myself, "he'll come during the morning because—when he's finally
ready—he'll want to get it over as early in the day as possible". Unfortunately of course I couldn't know which day. I didn't want to
get up unnecessarily early in the morning for perhaps a week. (*With
a rather pathetic gesture of apology for his appearance.*) So you'll have to
excuse . . . this.

(JANET *comes back.*)

JANET. Ah, there you are, Maurice. Has Colonel Forbes told you what
he has in mind?

MAURICE (*unsmiling as ever*). Yes, my dear. He's told me.

JANET. And what do you think?

MAURICE. What do I think?

JANET. What are you going to do?

MAURICE. Nothing.

COL. FORBES. The idea doesn't . . . I mean . . . it doesn't displease you?

MAURICE. Oh, it's nothing to do with that. It's out of the question,
that's all.

JANET. Are you sure?

MAURICE (*shaking his head*). It's impossible. I couldn't.

JANET. But surely, Maurice—

MAURICE (*very loudly and tormentedly*). No!

(*There is a long, embarrassed pause. No one moves. A rather
surprising change occurs in* JANET. *Her lips tremble and her hands*

fidget nervously together. She is a little like a child who has been harshly rebuked.)

JANET. I'm sorry, Maurice.

MAURICE. It's all right.

JANET. I didn't mean to annoy you.

MAURICE. All right, all right.

JANET. Please forgive me.

MAURICE. Yes, my dear—don't worry.

JANET *(quite distressed)*. No, but forgive me, Maurice. Say it. *(She seems totally unconcerned by the presence of the others and only desperately anxious to get back into* MAURICE's *good books.)*

MAURICE. I forgive you, Janet, it was nothing.

JANET *(very meekly)*. Yes, but kiss me. Forgive me properly.

MAURICE *(takes a step to* JANET *and kisses her forehead)*. Now Janet, there. It doesn't matter.

JANET *(as before)*. Thank you.

MAURICE *(as though to a child)*. Forget *all* about it.

JANET. Yes, Maurice.

MAURICE *(turns to* COLONEL FORBES*)*. Excuse the domestic scene, Colonel. We're all a little bit on edge in this house at times. And thank you, incidentally, for your very kind . . . offer.

COL. FORBES. Will you think it over?

(MAURICE *shakes his head.)*

It's a pity. I think I could pull something off.

MAURICE. I'm afraid it's too late for them to change their minds now. They had their own way—they turned me out. They wanted to ruin me—they said so—and they did.

COL. FORBES. Oh, come now . . .

MAURICE *(with a rather painful attempt at a smile)*. I used to be full of all sorts of idealistic notions! I used to tell myself that my job was to try to understand people so well . . . that I could help them to understand themselves a little better. And then this happened and I had a shock. I suddenly realized that I didn't understand people at *all!* I could find nothing but greed, vindictiveness, jealousy . . . meanness, cruelty, fear. Not in people who were ill. In people who were very well—and busily engaged in curing others! Well, we won't go into all that again. As far as Harley Street's concerned I'm not interested. And I never shall be.

COL. FORBES *(after a moment)*. Are you sure?

H.B.L.—B

MAURICE. Colonel Forbes, there are too many people in the profession who know. I've faced their vindictiveness. (*Sarcastically.*) I'm afraid their kindness would be *too* much.

COL. FORBES. Holt. You don't think this attitude is . . . rather weak?

MAURICE. Not at all. I deal with the world as it deals with me. People want to be tough? All right, I can be tough. It's a kind of strength.

(COLONEL FORBES *picks up his coat.*)

COL. FORBES. And all this was the fault of your step-brother?

MAURICE. Who told you that?

JANET. I did, Maurice. We were talking . . . before you came down.

MAURICE. Well, yes . . . it was.

COL. FORBES. It must be terrible for him.

MAURICE (*amazed*). Terrible for *him?* Good heavens! He doesn't give a damn.

COL. FORBES. He doesn't give a damn?

MAURICE. It didn't do him any harm, Colonel. Except financially. And he soon recovered from that.

COL. FORBES. I didn't mean financially.

MAURICE. No. I know you didn't. You meant the appalling remorse of having caused so much unhappiness. Well, there's no remorse. That's why I say he doesn't give a damn.

STELLA. He could have saved the situation anyway. He could have thrown in the resources of another of his companies to save the one that was in trouble.

MAURICE. All right, Stella.

STELLA. Oh, why not say it? (*To* COLONEL FORBES.) Of course that would have risked the second company as well! He felt that wouldn't be quite fair to the shareholders!

MAURICE. Quite. Well . . . never mind.

STELLA. Some years later we discovered that the shareholders in the second company were simply himself and his wife!

MAURICE (*angrily*). Stella!

STELLA. Well, it's true!

MAURICE. I'm sorry all this dirty linen should be washed in front of you, Colonel. It's not very pleasant for you.

(*A moment's pause. Then* COLONEL FORBES *holds out his hand.*)

COL. FORBES. Come and see us again soon.

MAURICE. With pleasure. Janet, will you ring for Brenda?

COL. FORBES. You too, Miss Holt.

STELLA. Thank you, Colonel.

(JANET *goes to the fireplace and rings the bell.* COLONEL·FORBES *puts on his coat.*)

MAURICE. I see they're still skating out there on the lake. Isn't it becoming rather dangerous? It was beginning to thaw yesterday.

COL. FORBES. I'm going to stop them tomorrow.

MAURICE. In nineteen sixty-four they left it a little late, I seem to remember.

COL. FORBES. In nineteen sixty-four I wasn't Chief Constable! (*He shakes hands with* JANET.)

(BRENDA *appears from kitchen no longer wearing her coat, and crosses with* COLONEL FORBES *to hall door.*)

Well . . . thank you all for receiving me damned interference with so much restraint!

JANET (*as he goes*). Good-bye, Colonel. My kind regards to Mrs. Forbes.

COL. FORBES (*disappearing*). Thank you. Good-bye, Miss Holt.

(BRENDA *sees* COLONEL FORBES *out, returns, closing hall door, crosses to kitchen door and goes out, closing it behind her.*)

JANET. What a kind man.

MAURICE. Very.

JANET. I don't understand why you're so worried about the skating, darling. That's twice you've mentioned it.

MAURICE. I don't think so.

JANET. You said yesterday that you didn't think Colin and Iris ought to walk across the ice to get from their house to this one.

MAURICE. Well we . . . don't want an accident, do we? Whatever our personal feelings may be about each other.

JANET. Has Colin agreed to the sale of the mill?

MAURICE. No.

JANET. What are you going to do?

MAURICE. Well, Janet, I rang him up this morning and offered to increase his share of the proceeds a little.

JANET. At the expense of ours?

MAURICE. Of course.

JANET. How much of our share did you offer him?

MAURICE. A thousand. I thought that might tempt him into closing with the offer.

JANET. Did it?

MAURICE. No.

JANET. But Maurice, dear, what *does* he want? The mill remains idle, rotting. Twenty thousand pounds! He's raving. Does he hope someone will offer more for it?

MAURICE. I don't know what he hopes. He goes on saying, as he always has done "I don't think we should sell".

JANET (*angrily*). He's doing it to spite you. He knows you need your share. That would be enough to make him refuse to sell.

MAURICE. I don't think there's much you can tell me and Stella about our dear stepbrother, Janet. We've had a lifetime of it.

JANET. I should like to talk to him.

MAURICE. I'd rather you didn't.

JANET. I might be able to persuade him . . . to touch him in some way. Don't you think so, Stella darling?

STELLA. I'm afraid I don't!

MAURICE. In any case I don't want you to try, Janet.

JANET. Then of course I shan't.

MAURICE. I'd like you to leave us now—I want to talk to Stella.

JANET. For long?

MAURICE. Just a few minutes.

JANET (*with a little sigh*). Very well.
                 (*She goes to the hall door. There she turns.*)
     Will you let me know when I can come back?

MAURICE (*patiently*). You can come back in a few minutes, Janet.

JANET. By the way, a man called. Looking for Colin. A Mr. Howard. Was that about it?

MAURICE. About what?

JANET. Well, about the sale of the Brocklebank Saw Mills.

MAURICE. I've no idea. What did he say?

JANET. Nothing. I told him it was the house on the other side of the lake.

MAURICE. Probably someone to whom Colin owes money.

JANET. Oh, how clever of you! That's exactly what he looked like!
     (*She withdraws, in her strange, submissive way. Left alone,*
     MAURICE *and* STELLA *stare at the door for a moment and then adopt a*
     tone both secretive and tense.)

MAURICE. All right. Now let's go over it all once again. And *think,* Stella. Think of every possible hitch.

STELLA. We've thought of everything.

MAURICE. We can't be too careful. Colin will come at about eight o'clock. (*Very thoughtfully.*) Eight o'clock. There's no danger of his bringing Iris. He hates her to be there when we're talking business. And, anyway, she's going to a whist drive. She won't be home before eleven.

(A moment's pause.)

STELLA. We shall have finished dinner by nine. I'll leave the table first. I'll prepare the coffee in here. Keep him in the dining-room until I call you.

MAURICE. How much of the stuff have you got?

STELLA. Two grains.

MAURICE. Where is it?

STELLA. Upstairs. I'll put it into my bag before dinner and bring it down.

(Another moment of silence. MAURICE *looks about, thinking, planning.* STELLA *keeps her eyes fixed on him.)*

MAURICE. Janet won't get back from the Davidsons' before ten-thirty. What about Brenda?

STELLA. She's going to the pictures. They come out at ten-fifteen. I've inquired.

MAURICE. Ten-fifteen.

STELLA. She gets the ten twenty-five bus. It puts her down at the gate at quarter to eleven.

MAURICE *(after a moment's thought)*. We're going to say he never turned up. What about the plates?

STELLA. I shall say I'm not well. I shall eat nothing. Three places will have been laid and only two of them used.

(Another pause.)

MAURICE. Now. About the rest. The pathways have all been swept. And there'll be no footprints on the ice anyway.

STELLA. Is it thawing still?

MAURICE. A little.

STELLA. What was the forecast?

MAURICE. A general thaw beginning this morning. It's perfect. The impression will be that he went through the ice on the way here. Just an ordinary accident.

STELLA. What about the pick-axe?

MAURICE. I'll leave it ready by the lake. At half-past ten or eleven no doubt Iris will telephone to ask when to expect him. If everything goes according to plan that will be the first inquiry. After that we must expect more and more questions. But we have only one answer to give. We waited for an hour and then had dinner. Will there be anyone in . . . over there . . . after he and Iris have left? Is it Maisie's night out?

STELLA. That is the only thing I can't be sure about.

MAURICE. Why not?

STELLA. It isn't her night off—officially. But as neither Colin nor Iris will be there she might easily go out.

MAURICE. You must ring up in case she's there. At nine o'clock. While you're making the coffee. We wouldn't sit here waiting without doing that. Talk normally. Say we can't think why he isn't here. What time did he leave . . . and so on. Put the gramophone on. Something loud. Keep it playing until you're ready for us. When the music stops I'll bring him in. I think that's all.

STELLA. There's one possibility we haven't considered, Maurice.

MAURICE (*quickly*). What?

STELLA. The possibility that Colin will come here tonight to *agree*.

MAURICE. To agree?

STELLA. To the sale of Brocklebank's.

MAURICE (*after a moment*). Well?

STELLA. He may.

MAURICE. Well of course he may!

STELLA. And in that event . . . ?

(She stops.)

MAURICE (*sarcastically*). In that event what? Let him go home after dinner? With our blessing? And then settle down to another ten years of this? Could you?

STELLA (*softly*). No.

MAURICE. Nor could I. I'm at the end. (*With a touch of desperation.*) I must have . . . somehow, from somewhere . . . money for Janet. And there's no other way of getting enough. Strange how this problem always comes back to Janet. You and I could go to the other end of the world and make a fresh start . . . on almost nothing. We *must*, Stella, we *must*. I have a right to that, surely. To work again . . . to function. It's insane otherwise. But as long as Janet and I are roped together . . . no . . . Janet must stand on her own feet.

STELLA. I don't think Janet *wants* to stand on her own feet.

MAURICE. Of course she doesn't want to . . . but that doesn't mean she won't be able to . . . once she has no choice. Good God, if I were dead Janet would marry someone else within a year . . . and settle down to a healthy, normal life, I'm sure of it. And the same

thing would happen if you and I could only go away . . . once
we were out of reach . . . gone for good. But I can't go away and
leave her with insufficient means . . . that's out of the question.

STELLA (*very softly and thoughtfully*). After I leave the table . . . coffee
. . . telephone call . . . you'll have to keep him talking for five or
six minutes.

MAURICE. We shan't move till the music stops.

STELLA. I think . . .
          (*Hearing a sound* MAURICE *holds up his hand and interrupts her.
          They listen. After a second* JANET *comes back.*)

JANET. Is it all right, now?

MAURICE. Of course, Janet.

STELLA (*casually*). Darling, what time do you have to be at the
Davidsons' tonight?

JANET. Oh . . . I don't think I'm going.
          (*They both turn to her in some astonishment.*)

MAURICE. Why not?

JANET. Did you want me to go?

MAURICE. I said why have you changed your mind, Janet?

JANET. Well, I decided that as you and Stella weren't going it didn't
interest me. I'd rather be with you. Aren't you pleased?

MAURICE. It isn't that, Janet dear. I think Stella and I must talk to
Colin alone.

JANET. But why, Maurice? I know all about it and Colin *knows* I
know all about it. Why keep me out of it?

MAURICE. I just don't like you to be involved in things like this,
darling. It's a sordid, depressing family affair. It's for me and
Stella to deal with. For our sins we've been dealing with Colin all
our lives. We're used to it.

JANET. Yes, and he's always got the better of you. It might be a good
thing if I joined in. Anyway, I can't go now. I've told Joyce not to
expect me.

STELLA. But when did you do that, dear?

JANET. This morning. After breakfast. I rang her up.

MAURICE (*very gently*). Well now, Janet. You must ring her up again.
(*Taking her hands in his.*) Tell her you've changed your mind once
more. She won't be surprised. You often do that. And you'll go
there to dinner as arranged. And Stella and I will have had a dreary
evening and you'll come back at bedtime and make us laugh. You
see?

JANET. But I don't want to do that.

MAURICE. Are you sure you don't?

JANET. Positive.

MAURICE. I think you're wrong.

JANET. Surely I ought to know what I want to do, darling.

MAURICE. But you said yesterday you were looking forward to it. It's always fun there, you said. Good dinner. Amusing people. Probably some lovely music.

JANET. Well, yes . . . I would have enjoyed it, of course.

MAURICE. And what about Roland Young? Isn't he going to be there after all?

JANET. I imagine so.

MAURICE. Well . . . but you wanted to meet him.

JANET. Yes. Yes, I did.

MAURICE. And you do still. Don't you?

JANET. I . . . it would amuse me, yes. Only . . .

MAURICE. Only what, my dear?

JANET. Well, I don't know . . . I thought I didn't really care terribly . . . and I thought you might prefer me to stay.

MAURICE. No, no. I've told you what I would like. I'd like you to enjoy your evening and then come and tell me all about it. I should love that. Be so amusing.

JANET. It *is* a good idea. How stupid I've been.

MAURICE. It doesn't matter. Just ring up.

JANET. Do you think I can? Again?

MAURICE. But of course.

JANET. Yes. I suppose I can. Very well. I will.

MAURICE. I should do it now.

JANET. I can't yet. Joyce was just going out. She won't be back until lunch-time.

(STELLA *is looking into the garden.*)

STELLA. Good heavens! Here's Colin! (*She opens the french windows.*)

MAURICE (*in surprise*). Colin? What's he doing here at this time of the day?

(*After another moment* COLIN *comes in from the garden. He is a striking-looking individual but not very pleasing. Short, slight and prematurely bald, he has a clever face; clever but devoid of kindness. He is dressed rather formally, and not at all suitably for the country, in striped trousers, a black coat and Homburg hat.*)

COLIN. Good morning, all!

JANET. How are you, Colin?

COLIN. I'm well, Janet. I trust you are.

MAURICE. What do you want?

COLIN. All right, Maurice. Try to sound a little more genial. (*He takes out a cigarette case and offers* JANET *a cigarette. She accepts and he lights both hers and his with his lighter.*)

JANET. Is Iris not with you?

COLIN. She'll be here in a few minutes. We're lunching in Town. I was in a hurry to talk to you so I came across the lake.

JANET (*taking the cigarette*). Thank you. Maurice thinks it's getting dangerous . . . you ought to come round by the road.

COLIN. It's very kind of Maurice to think of my safety.

MAURICE. You must look very curious fidgeting across the ice in those clothes. Like some singular beetle nervously crossing a bathroom floor.

COLIN. That is a very affectionate and brotherly remark, Maurice, and I want you to know that I appreciate it. However, let me come to the point. I believe you're acquainted with Colonel and Mrs. Forbes.

MAURICE. Slightly.

COLIN. Slightly? Surely Janet and Mrs. Forbes are quite good friends.

JANET. Yes, I know her.

COLIN. Do you like her?

JANET. Very much.

COLIN. Good. And I'm sure she likes you. Now. It so happens that Mrs. Forbes is on the Council.

MAURICE. What is all this leading up to?

COLIN. Would you like to ask her to do something for me, Janet?

MAURICE. No. She would not.

COLIN. Let Janet answer for herself, Maurice . . . for once. You don't even know what I'm asking yet.

JANET. What is it?

COLIN (*to* MAURICE). When you know what it is you may be in favour. I rather suspect you will be.

MAURICE. Why?

COLIN. You remember the shares I gave you in the Majestic Cinema in the High Street?

MAURICE. Gave?

COLIN. Well . . . the shares I enabled you to acquire. Shall I put it that way?

MAURICE. What about them?

COLIN. Still holding them, aren't you?

MAURICE. I can't sell them. I wish I could.

COLIN. There's still a chance they may be worth something one day, Maurice. But not if the Council grants a licence next Monday morning for the construction of a much bigger cinema with a café and dance hall bang on the opposite side of the street. And I happen to know that such a licence is being asked for.

MAURICE. *How* do you know?

COLIN. Never mind. I do.

MAURICE. And you think that Janet and I can help to get it stopped. Is that it?

COLIN. Well, Janet's a friend of Mrs. Forbes. And Mrs. Forbes is on the Council. Seems a pity if one has influence not to use it.

MAURICE. It's a shame you didn't come a little sooner. Colonel Forbes was here. You could have persuaded *him* to ask Mrs. Forbes. He'd have been only too pleased, I'm sure. He's the Chief Constable, you know.

COLIN. Come now, don't start preaching, Maurice. Business is business.

MAURICE. Well, Janet, do you see what's required of you?

JANET. But it's simply monstrous. You mean you want her to try to stop these people getting their licence just because it's to your advantage?

STELLA. Really, Colin! Can't you ever do *anything* straightforward?

JANET. But even if I *would* ask her she'd never do it.

COLIN. But I'm trying to help you all. Maurice has an interest at stake.

MAURICE. And you thought that would make us rush to the rescue, did you?

COLIN. I didn't think it would make you all stand there moralizing, I must admit.

MAURICE. Well, you'd better go and think up something else.

COLIN. No, Maurice. It's you who'd better do that. And by this evening if you don't mind.

MAURICE. Why?

COLIN. I've got much more in this than you have, Maurice. I'm in it to the tune of twelve thousand pounds. And unfortunately my partner has even more to lose. I have to be able to ring him up to-night—tonight, notice, not tomorrow—and tell him that Mrs. Forbes has been approached. Not will be, notice, has been. Otherwise he's going to save himself and put me in the soup. And if you don't help I'm afraid you'll be in the soup too. Because you know what I'll do? I'll sell this house. I'll have to.

JANET. Oh Colin, for God's sake! Haven't we been through enough? Hasn't Maurice . . .

MAURICE. Keep calm, Janet, keep calm.

COLIN. On the other hand . . . if you agree . . . I might show my gratitude this evening by consenting to the sale of that damned saw mill. And you and Stella will be ten thousand pounds richer. That a bargain?

STELLA. I should call it blackmail.

JANET. Why don't you agree to selling the mill anyway and buy your partner off with your share of that?

COLIN. Because it wouldn't be enough.

STELLA (angrily). You're an obstinate fool, Colin! The place will never work again and we shall never get another offer. It's only because of its position and the machinery that we've had this one.

COLIN. Well, we'll talk about that tonight. You do what I want. And maybe I'll do what you want.

MAURICE (bursting out). How the devil can we? You think that everyone's a crook because you are. You think we're all . . .

COLIN (very loudly). All right, all right! No need to be offensive!

(A moment's pause.)

MAURICE. You're so stupid, Colin. Why should Mrs. Forbes want to do such a thing?

COLIN. Well, if she knew this project would ruin a good friend of hers . . . wouldn't that mean anything to her?

JANET. We can't be turned out of this house, Colin, we can't. We've lost everything else. Where shall we go? What are we to do?·

COLIN. Nobody's turning you out, Janet. It's just circumstances.

MAURICE (angrily). This house belongs to me and Stella, by right! Father always intended that and your mother knew it. (Sarcastically.) But of course her one ewe lamb had to have everything.

COLIN. But I put it at your disposal, Maurice. I . . .

MAURICE. You should have transferred it to us legally. In any case this house isn't going to be taken away from us because of some sordid, financial stupidity of yours, Colin. I'll see to that.

COLIN. I'm afraid it is, you know—unless you do what I ask.

(The hall door opens and IRIS appears. She is a woman whose age is not easy to guess. No doubt she is still in her forties. She is such a *tormented little person—so constantly distraught—that she might be younger than she looks. At the moment she is white with anger. She is dressed in black, very nicely, for Town. She is chic and well made up.)* Ah, it's dear old Iris! Got here at last!

IRIS *(furiously).* Shut up! *(She goes to JANET.)* Good morning, Janet, darling. Good morning, Maurice, Stella. *(Kissing JANET.)* Are you all right, darling?

JANET *(gently).* Iris . . . what's the matter? You've been crying. *(She speaks very tenderly and puts an arm round her.)*

IRIS. Oh . . . can't you imagine?

COLIN *(with a laugh).* Poor old Iris! She was frightened to walk across the ice! So she had to go all the way round by the road! Half a mile . . . instead of a hundred yards!

IRIS *(furiously).* I was *not* frightened!

COLIN *(jeering).* Of course you were!

IRIS. I *wasn't!* I told you I didn't want to walk across the ice in these shoes.

COLIN. It's quite easy if you put your feet down the way I told you. *(To the others.)* I even had Burton sprinkle some gravel to make it easy for her.

IRIS. It's quite easy for you, in your ridiculous galoshes!

COLIN. You were frightened!

IRIS. I was *not* frightened!

COLIN. All right, all right! I expect they believe you even if I don't!

IRIS *(almost in tears).* If you weren't too mean to buy chains for the wheels we could use the car!

COLIN. I don't care to drive in three feet of snow, chains or no chains.

IRIS. No! You're frightened!

COLIN *(angrily).* Now shut up!

IRIS. If you had any breeding you'd have walked round with me. But of course you've only got the manners of a farm-hand!

COLIN *(at the top of his voice).* I said shut up! *(Softly.)* Silly bitch.

MAURICE. If you don't mind I think I'll go and dress. I don't enjoy the way you talk to your wife, Colin.

COLIN. See you tonight.

(MAURICE goes out up right.)

Now stop it, Iris. You're only going to spoil your make-up.

IRIS. Oh, shut up! Don't speak to me! You're just a beast!

(COLIN takes a step towards her.)

(Hysterically.) Yes, go on! Hit me! Hit me in front of them like you do at home! There isn't a man here now! It's quite safe!

(*Turning to* JANET.) Oh God, I don't know why I go on with it! I could easily make an end of it . . . why didn't I do that long ago?
JANET (*putting her arms round her*). Iris darling, you mustn't talk like that.
IRIS. But I *could*, darling. I could so easily. I even have something. Why *should* one go on with a life that isn't worth living?
COLIN (*looking at his watch*). Well, are you coming, Iris?
JANET. She's coming in a few minutes when she feels calmer. (*Softly, to* IRIS.) Don't cry, my dear. (*To the others.*) Go into the other room for a minute.

      (STELLA *and* COLIN *go towards the hall door.*)

COLIN. You can have five minutes to pull yourself together, Iris. If you're not ready then I shall go without you.
IRIS (*in* JANET's *arms*). I wish you would.
COLIN (*at the door*). What did you say, Iris?
JANET. Nothing, Colin. Please go.

      (COLIN *and* STELLA *go out, closing the door.*)

Now, darling . . . sit down. I'm going to give you something to drink.

      (IRIS *sits down on the sofa and opens her bag to look into the mirror in the flap.* JANET *crosses to where there are drinks on a side-table and makes a small whisky and soda for her.*)

How did it start this time?
IRIS (*emphatically*). I've told you how it started. I simply didn't want to teeter across a hundred yards of ice in these shoes, gravel or no gravel. Who would? Then he said I was a silly bitch and left me to walk all the way round by the road alone. But it's always the same. The slightest thing is enough. We can't go on any longer. I can't. My nerves won't stand it, Janet, they really won't.

      (JANET *comes back to* IRIS *with the drink.*)

JANET. Iris, I want to ask you something. Here, drink this.
IRIS. Yes, dear, put it there.

      (IRIS *is beginning to repair the damage to her make-up.* JANET *puts the glass on a small table close to her and sits beside her on the sofa.*)

JANET. What did you mean just now when you said you had something?
IRIS. Had something?
JANET. You said "I could easily put an end to it all. I have something".
IRIS. It's quite true.
JANET *What* have you?

IRIS. I have peace, Janet˙ . . . the possibility of endless peace.
JANET. Yes, but what *is* it, Iris?

> (*A long pause.* IRIS *passes her mouth slowly from side to side on the lipstick.*)

Iris, tell me.
IRIS. You promise you won't tell anyone?
JANET. I promise.
IRIS. It's morphine, actually.
JANET. You have some morphine? Enough for that?
IRIS (*putting away her lipstick*). More than enough.
JANET. Where did you get it from?
IRIS. From Nurse Thomson.
JANET (*horrified*). Nurse Thomson has been supplying you with morphine?
IRIS. Oh, only a little at a time. But I've saved it up.
JANET (*softly*). Iris! How much have you got?
IRIS. One capsule will relieve pain. Four will make you sleep. Twelve would kill you! (*Contentedly.*) And I have sixteen. (*She stares at* JANET *for a moment and then, suddenly, goes off into peals of laughter.*)
JANET. Iris! Iris! Stop!
IRIS (*controlling herself*). I'm sorry! You looked so scared!
JANET (*warmly*). Well of course I'm scared . . . walking around talking about suicide with sixteen capsules of . . . where are they, these things?
IRIS. At home. Do you think I carry them about with me?
JANET. You must give them to me, Iris.
IRIS. To *you!* Of *all* people!
JANET. Oh, you needn't worry . . . that's all over.
IRIS. All the same . . . I certainly wouldn't give you my morphine.
JANET. You could, you know. Quite safely.
IRIS. You say that, Janet. But you did try, didn't you?
JANET. Yes. I did. Twice.
IRIS. Well then . . .
JANET. But Iris, dear, the means of killing ourselves are all around us, all the time. I need only take the boat into the wide part of the lake and flood it. I couldn't swim half the distance back. I have only to turn on the gas fire in the spare room, or simply take Maurice's revolver from his desk . . . or I could pull the electric fire into the bath and electrocute myself. But I don't. Because I don't any longer

see it as a solution. I don't approve of it. I think it's wrong. That's what stops me, darling, not the fact that I haven't got sixteen capsules of morphine in the house.

IRIS. In that case the absence of morphine in the house wouldn't stop me. So there's no point in my giving it to you, is there? (*She takes a drink.*)

JANET. Well, I . . . all the same . . . I wish you would, Iris.

IRIS. You have more confidence in yourself than in me, have you?

JANET. Well, of course I have. You don't think of suicide as I do. You probably think of it the way I *used* to. And you're very impulsive, Iris darling. (*Taking her hands.*) With those things in the house you might do something foolish . . . in the agitation of the moment . . . something you wouldn't do at all if you had to spend as much as half a minute thinking of some other way.

IRIS. How happy are *you,* Janet? You and Maurice.

JANET. Don't you know?

IRIS. You seem to be happy. Anyway, in comparison with us.

JANET. We're not. I sometimes think we could be . . . if Maurice could be happy with anyone. But we've been through far too much. Things have been spoiled for us.

(IRIS *puts down her glass and rises.*)

IRIS. But why go on with something if it isn't a success?

JANET. I suppose as long as Maurice is alive I'll have to go on with it.

IRIS (*putting on her gloves*). So it isn't because of happiness that you cling to life.

JANET (*jumping up vehemently*). Oh, please forget what I tried to do! I don't cling to life, Iris. I *live.* I think it's our duty to live the life that's been laid out for us . . . whether it's happy or not. Your unhappiness and mine aren't the beginning and the end of everything. The world's a very unhappy place. No doubt for lots of people death is the only possible release from sheer agony . . . like going to sleep when you're worn out and wretched. I've always thought that and I still think it. But now I also think another thing. I think one simply mustn't soil oneself with something cowardly and abject. It's dishonest, cheating, trying not to face up to things, That's what I think of suicide. I'm horribly ashamed of what I did. I shall certainly never think of *that* way out again.

(IRIS *kisses her.*)

IRIS. I wish that you and Maurice were very happy. I think that would restore my faith in things.

JANET. I want you to make me a promise.

IRIS. What?

JANET (*taking hold of her*). Promise me that however desperate you feel you won't do anything without first talking to me. Promise?

(*The hall door opens and* COLIN *appears.*)

COLIN (*loudly*). Iris!

IRIS. Yes . . . I'm coming.

COLIN. We're going to be late.

IRIS. All right, don't shout! (*Hastily kissing* JANET *again.*) Good-bye, darling . . .

JANET (*catching at her*). Promise, Iris! I won't let you go!

IRIS (*dragging herself free*). Darling, I must!

COLIN (*at the same time*). Oh, come on!

JANET. Iris! Promise you'll do what I say!

IRIS (*as she goes out*). All right! Thank you. Forgive me.

(IRIS *and* COLIN *go out, leaving the door open.* BRENDA *comes in from kitchen.*)

BRENDA. Excuse me, ma'am, but about tonight.

JANET. What about tonight, Brenda?

BRENDA. Is it so you'll not be here after all?

JANET. Oh, that reminds me. I must telephone. No, Brenda, I'm going out.

BRENDA. So there'll be three?

(JANET *goes to the telephone.*)

JANET. Yes, Brenda. Mr. Colin will be coming. Lay the table for three before you go.

(BRENDA *goes to collect* IRIS's *glass.* JANET *dials a number.*)

BRENDA. I'll take the glass while I'm here. Poor Mrs. Colin . . . she was really upset. I thought something awful had happened.

JANET (*into telephone*). Is Mrs. Davidson there? Oh, all right . . . I'll call again . . . no, it doesn't matter. Thank you. (*Putting down the telephone.*) What time is it, Brenda?

BRENDA. I suppose it'll be about half after twelve, ma'am. Lunch in half an hour. Will that be all right?

JANET. Yes, Brenda. Thank you.

BRENDA. Thank you, ma'am.

(BRENDA *returns to kitchen, closing the door. At the same moment* MR. HOWARD *appears at the french windows and taps on the glass.* JANET *sees him and at once goes and opens for him.*

HOWARD *is a curious looking man—neither young nor old—very slovenly in his dress. He wears a very old, blue overcoat and a worn silk scarf with some vague, public school stripe in it. He has no hat and his hair looks as ungroomed as the rest of him; perhaps a gentleman who has fallen on hard times.*)

JANET. So you're back again. Come in.

HOWARD. Thank you. (*He comes in, looking around him.*)

JANET. If you're still looking for Mr. Colin Holt, I'm afraid you've missed him.

HOWARD. Yes.

JANET. You found the house though, did you?

HOWARD. Thank you . . . yes . . . I did.

JANET. I'm surprised you didn't meet him on the way. He came here. But of course you wouldn't know him, would you?

HOWARD. I didn't meet anyone who could have been him.

JANET. Oh, of course. He came across the lake.

HOWARD. Across the lake?

JANET. It's very narrow just here. They use it as a short cut while it's frozen.

HOWARD. I met a woman . . . in black . . . who seemed to be in tears.

JANET. I'm sorry to tell you that that was his wife.

HOWARD. Nothing seriously wrong, I hope?

JANET. No. Just a domestic explosion.

HOWARD. Oh yes.

JANET. Will you smoke? (*She offers a cigarette from a wooden box on the table.*)

HOWARD. Thank you.

(*She lights it for him.*)

Well. He seems to be a difficult man to find.

JANET. I'm awfully sorry about it. Have you been chasing him like this for long?

HOWARD. Not very long.

(*The conversation seems to flag and* HOWARD *makes no attempt to renew it.*)

H.B.L.—C

JANET. Well . . .

(HOWARD *looks at her interrogatively.*)

(*With an uncomfortable little laugh.*) I . . . that seems to be all we can do for the moment, doesn't it?

HOWARD (*after a second*). Yes.

JANET. He's gone up to Town, you see, now.

HOWARD. Yes?

JANET. He'll be back this evening, though.

HOWARD. Ah!

JANET. He's coming here for dinner.

HOWARD. Ah?

JANET. It isn't my business, of course, Mr. Howard, but am I right in thinking it's about . . . money?

HOWARD. Well, as a matter of fact, yes.

JANET. You could come here tonight. Oh no. Perhaps you'd better not. My husband will be talking business with him. You'd better call at his house again tomorrow.

HOWARD. Well, thank you. I'll try to do what you suggest.

(*Another pause.* JANET *fidgets now a little, wondering how to get rid of him.*)

JANET. Well, Mr. Howard . . .

(HOWARD *looks at her again. He reflects for a moment. Then suddenly.*)

HOWARD. Oh, I'm sorry. You're busy. Good morning, Mrs. Holt. And thank you. I'll go this way . . . don't trouble. (*He goes to the french windows. Then—*) There are plenty of trains up to Town from here?

JANET. Every fifteen minutes.

HOWARD. Perhaps we shall meet again.

JANET. I do hope so.

HOWARD. If not today, tomorrow. If not tomorrow the next day.

JANET (*with a bewildered little laugh*). Yes.

HOWARD. Good morning.

(HOWARD *goes out slowly, closing the french windows after him. Then he turns up the collar of his coat and shuffles off.* JANET *stares for a moment. Then she goes to the telephone and dials a number.*)

JANET. Hello? Oh Joyce, dear, Janet. I called before but you weren't
back. Joyce, would you let me change my mind and come after
all? . . . no, only me. The others can't still . . . you *are* an
angel! I decided I couldn't bear to miss it after all! Seven o'clock
then! Good-bye! Oh, Joyce, Joyce! Just one thing . . . if I suddenly decide I want to run away early you won't mind, will you?
. . . **You *are* an angel.**

THE CURTAIN FALLS.

ACT TWO

The scene is the same. The time is the evening of the same day.

When the curtain rises no one is present and the room is lighted by several lamps and by the glow of the fire. The gramophone is playing the first movement of Schumann's Piano Concerto. After a moment the hall door opens and STELLA *comes in carrying a tray of coffee things. She puts the tray on a low table in front of the fire. She is wearing a wine-coloured silk blouse and a black skirt and is generally much more groomed than she was in Act One.*

As soon as she has put down the tray she crosses to the telephone. But, as she does so, the other door opens and MAURICE *appears. He is wearing a shabby, tweed suit. He closes the door behind him, keeping one hand on the knob, and speaks in a loud whisper above the music.*

MAURICE. Stella! Stella!

STELLA. What? Wait! (*She goes quickly to the gramophone and turns down the volume.*) What's happened?

MAURICE. It's too late! It's too late!

STELLA (*nervously*). What's the matter with you?

MAURICE. We should have finished dinner at nine!

STELLA. What time is it now?

MAURICE. Twenty-five past.

STELLA. There's still an hour. No one will be back yet.

MAURICE (*softly*). I don't know . . . it seems dangerous now.

STELLA. Keep your head, Maurice! Go back to him! I'm going to telephone!

MAURICE. For God's sake be quick!

(*He goes out again, closing the door.* STELLA *goes to the telephone, dials a number and waits. Her glance is constantly drawn towards the door through which* MAURICE *has disappeared.*)

STELLA. Oh, Maisie, is that you? Is Mr. Holt there? (*After a pause.*) I don't understand . . . he was supposed to be coming here for dinner . . . no, he hasn't . . . I don't know . . . unless he's forgotten about it . . . it does seem strange, doesn't it? Well, Maisie,

if he comes back ask him to call us. Madam isn't there, is she? . . .
All right, thank you, good-bye.

(*She replaces the receiver. For a moment she stands quite still,
thinking. Then she goes to the gramophone again and very gradually
increases the volume. With the music now playing very loudly she goes
across to the tray of coffee things. Kneeling beside it she pours out one
cup of coffee. Then she takes her bag from a chair close by, opens it and
takes out a very small box. She opens this in turn and carefully pours
the contents into the cup of coffee, after which she drops the box into
the fire. Then she rises, goes to the gramophone and cuts it off abruptly.*

*Going to the french windows, she makes sure that the curtains are
completely closed. Then she goes back to the coffee tray and pours out a
second cup.* MAURICE *and* COLIN *now come in from up right.*)

MAURICE (*as they enter*). But what about Iris?
COLIN (*angrily*). The question of Iris doesn't come into it! Iris and I
are through!

(MAURICE *stops and stares at him in surprise.*)

MAURICE. Since when?
COLIN. Since this evening.

(STELLA *rises, holding the cup of coffee.*)

MAURICE. Why? What happened this evening?
COLIN. We had the biggest bloody row we've ever had in our lives.

(*He takes the cup of coffee from* STELLA, *who stares at him for a
second or two before recollecting herself sufficiently to turn and pick up
the second cup which she gives to* MAURICE. *During the following lines
she also hands them sugar.*)

MAURICE. Iris has done a great deal for you, Colin.
COLIN. And of course I've done nothing for her, have I? I've supported
her for fifteen years, I know that.
MAURICE. Well, why shouldn't you?
COLIN. I've had enough of her.
MAURICE. What do you mean exactly when you say that you and Iris
are through?
COLIN. I mean I've asked her to be kind enough to go and live some-
where else.
MAURICE. Where?
COLIN. I don't know where. It doesn't interest me. She'll go back to
that surly father of hers, I suppose.
MAURICE. In fact you've simply turned her out . . . is that it?

COLIN. If you want to put it like that, yes. (*He takes the first drink of coffee. STELLA and MAURICE, sitting on the sofa, stare at him as though fascinated.*)
(*Sarcastically.*) Done a great deal for me! Iris! Huh! Nobody's done a great deal for me, let me tell you, except myself.

MAURICE. And you've never done anything for anyone else.
(COLIN *takes another drink of coffee.*)

COLIN. What happened this morning when I asked you people to do a little thing for me? An ordinary everyday bit of business diplomacy. You started moralizing . . . as usual. I know you. You'd let me go bust without raising a finger. And what do you expect *me* to do in return? Agree to the sale of the Brocklebank Saw Mills? So that you can all sit back and do nothing for another few years? Huh! Not likely. (*He drains his coffee cup and then puts the cup and saucer down on the table. He is standing at centre, close to them.*) Well, I've got out of some tight corners before now. It's been tough, oh yes. But this time it's going to be tough for you as well. And don't say I didn't warn you and give you a chance to avoid it. Don't be too sorry for yourselves. Because that's always been the trouble with you two. You're too sorry for yourselves.
(*He takes out his cigarette case and extracts a cigarette from it.*)
Same with Iris. She's another. Whining and whimpering. That's all she ever does. Well, she's going to whimper to someone else now. If she can find anyone to listen. (*He puts the cigarette case back and begins to feel in his other pockets for his lighter, the cigarette between his lips. MAURICE and STELLA, their eyes fixed on him, do not move a muscle.*)
"What am I going to live on?" she kept on asking. "I don't know," I said. "Maybe you're going to have to go out to work like everyone else," I said. She didn't like that. Got a match?
(MAURICE *begins to move slowly. But suddenly it becomes unnecessary as COLIN finds his lighter.*)
Oh, it's all right. (*Suddenly he stands quite still, puts the lighter back into his pocket, takes the cigarette from his lips, drops it on to an ashtray and places one hand on his head, swaying.*) God . . . I think I'm going to faint.
(*He groans and leans forward. MAURICE, galvanized at last into action, leaps to his feet and catches him as he is falling. He supports him for a moment, bracing himself for a further effort. Then he gets him on to the sofa. COLIN slumps over the arm of it, inert. MAURICE and*

STELLA *stare at him for a second or two.* STELLA, *as though she were feeling slightly sick, sinks on to the edge of a chair.* Then they are startled by the sudden ringing of the telephone.)

STELLA. What do we do?

MAURICE. Answer it!

STELLA (*shakily*). I don't think I can.

(MAURICE *goes to the telephone and lifts the receiver.*)

MAURICE. Yes? . . . No. I'm afraid he isn't . . . Yes, we expected him for dinner but he didn't come. Who is it speaking?

(*There is a click and the burring of the dialling tone as the other person hangs up.* MAURICE *does the same and remains there with his hand on the instrument.*)

STELLA. Who was it?

MAURICE. Don't know. He hung up. Quick . . . come on.

(*He goes out to the hall.* STELLA *remains where she is, staring at the lifeless body of* COLIN. *After a few seconds* MAURICE *comes back, carrying his overcoat. He, too, stands looking at* COLIN *while he puts it on.*)

STELLA. I think I'd better come with you.

MAURICE (*rapidly*). No, no. I can manage. You stay here in case anything happens. Don't forget. If anyone phones I'm listening to something I don't want to miss on the radio and I'll call them back.

(*He has now buttoned up his coat. He puts the lights out so that the scene is only lit by the glow from the fire. Then he goes quickly to the french windows and, after dragging back the curtains, opens them. Outside it is very dark. He steps outside, looks up and then comes in again.*)

It's quite dark. It's perfect. Let's get on with it.

STELLA (*suddenly*). Listen!

(*They stand absolutely still for a moment.*)

MAURICE. What's the matter?

(STELLA *shakes her hand to stop him from speaking and again they listen.*)

STELLA (*softly, in horror*). Maurice! There's someone in the house!

(*Suddenly that part of the garden immediately outside the french windows is brilliantly floodlit. She gasps and clutches* MAURICE'S *arm.*)

It's the kitchen!

(MAURICE *goes quickly to the french windows, shuts them and draws the curtains. Then he turns to her.*)

MAURICE. Go and see who it is.

(STELLA *goes out quickly to the kitchen.* MAURICE *puts the desk-light on and waits, absolutely still, facing the door. There is very little light.*

After a few seconds STELLA *comes back, closes the door and lean against it, shaken with fear.*)

STELLA. Oh God. Brenda's in the kitchen.

MAURICE (*in a furious whisper*). You fool! I told you it was too late!

STELLA. But it's barely ten o'clock!

(BRENDA'S *voice is heard off.*)

BRENDA (*off*). Miss Stella?

STELLA (*paralysed with fright*). What shall I do?

MAURICE (*very calmly*). Pull yourself together! Go to her.

(STELLA *goes out again, closing the door.* MAURICE *immediately goes to the built-in cupboard and opens it. Then he returns rapidly to the sofa, drags* COLIN *from it and half carries, half drags him to the cupboard, deposits him inside it and shuts the door. At the same moment* STELLA *comes back. She is very white.* MAURICE *takes* COLIN'S *coat and hat from a chair, up left, and puts these into the cupboard also. Then he turns to* STELLA.)

STELLA. She didn't like the film. Came out half-way through and caught the nine-forty bus.

(*A moment's pause. She touches the switch and the other lights come up again.*)

MAURICE. Came in by the side door?

STELLA. Must have done.

MAURICE. What's she doing now?

(*Before* STELLA *can reply* BRENDA *taps on the door and comes in. She has taken off her overcoat and is putting a white apron over her "going out" clothes, which are nice and in good taste. She talks gently in her slow, thin, but curiously musical voice, blissfully unaware of the anxiety she causes.*)

BRENDA. Now is there anything you're needing here before I start to clear the dining-room? Oh, you've got no logs for the fire. I'll go and get you some.

MAURICE. You needn't trouble, Brenda.

BRENDA. Oh, it's no trouble. You must have logs for the fire. Have you finished with the coffee things? (*She begins to collect the coffee cups.*) And where's Mr. Colin? Didn't he come after all?

MAURICE. No. He . . . he didn't come.

BRENDA. Imagine that! At least I hope he had the kindness to let you know.

STELLA. No . . . he, he simply, he just didn't turn up.

BRENDA. Surely you're not going out, Mr. Maurice.

MAURICE. No, I'm . . . I'm not going out. (*Unbuttoning his coat.*) I just went as far as the gate to see if Mr. Colin was coming.

BRENDA (*cooing away peacefully*). And he just left you waiting and never telephoned. Oh dear, oh dear. Oh, but that's shocking, really shocking, not to have more consideration for others. (*She puts the two coffee cups on to the tray and picks it up.*)

STELLA (*recovering her poise a little*). I'll wash up, Brenda . . . I expect you're tired.

BRENDA (*with a sweet, tinkling little laugh*). Oh, why should I be tired, Miss Stella? I'm too old to go to bed at ten o'clock! I'd never get to sleep! Oh no, I'll clear everything up nice and tidy for the morning. (*Laughing to herself as she goes.*) No, I'm not tired! Imagine that! (*Exit to kitchen with the coffee tray.*)

MAURICE (*as soon as the door has closed*). You'd better go and keep her talking. See she does wash up, while I get away.

STELLA. You can't go past the kitchen window while she's in and out. There are no curtains. She'd see you.

MAURICE. Can't you keep her talking in the dining-room? Well, do something, for God's sake! Don't stand there trembling!

STELLA. Don't be a fool, Maurice! It isn't my fault she's come back early.

MAURICE (*at the same time*). I might have known you'd lose your head and make a mess of it.

(BRENDA *comes gently ambling back with two small logs.*)

BRENDA. Only two logs left. I must go out to the shed and get some more.

STELLA. I think that'll be enough for this evening, Brenda.

(BRENDA *kneels down in front of the fire and attends to it methodically.*)

BRENDA. Oh, we mustn't have you catching cold. No, I'll make you a good fire.

STELLA. I don't think you ought to go out to the wood shed in the dark, Brenda.

BRENDA. Oh, that's all right, m'dear. I'm used to it. (*Gently laughing again.*) I may be getting on but I've eyes like a young cat.

MAURICE. All the same I think I'll go, Brenda. I have my coat on.

BRENDA. Such a ridiculous picture! You wouldn't imagine. Sometimes I wonder who thinks of these things. (*She blows gently into the fire. Then she carefully puts the logs on. As she does so.*) Such a silly story. It was all about a rich girl who pretended to be poor in order to get a really nice husband. (*Sweeping the fireplace.*) As though the poor were all happily married. (*Laughing gently.*) Oh dear, oh dear! It was awfully silly!

MAURICE. You can tell us about that in the morning, Brenda.

BRENDA (*rising*). I will if I can remember it so long! (*Going to the door.*) But I expect I'll have forgotten all about it after a good sleep! (*She goes out, still laughing softly.*)

MAURICE. Go to the kitchen. Keep her talking. (*He buttons his coat up again.*)

STELLA. What are you going to do?

MAURICE. I'll have to go by the front. Whatever happens, don't let her come out of the kitchen. Wait. (*Softly.*) Listen. Janet's back. Listen, someone's with her.

(*They turn as the hall door opens and* JANET *comes in. She is wearing a black, evening coat over a décolletée dress, also black. She is not expensively dressed but she is dressed with chic and looks extremely nice, especially as she has had an amusing, stimulating evening. Her eyes are sparkling. She is accompanied by* COLONEL FORBES, *who is wearing a dinner jacket under a loose tweed overcoat.*)

JANET. Hello! Here we are!

MAURICE (*softly*). Janet!

JANET. Colonel and Mrs. Forbes were there. They were kind enough to bring me home. We took Mrs. Forbes back first. She had a headache.

COL. FORBES (*cheerfully*). Evening!

STELLA (*mechanically*). Good evening.

JANET. You were silly not to come. Joyce gave us a wonderful dinner and we had champagne! We had a lovely time, didn't we, Colonel!

COL. FORBES. Indeed we did.

(JANET *takes off her wrap.* BRENDA *comes in from the kitchen with more logs.*)

BRENDA. Oh, good evening, ma'am. I'm glad you're safely back. Is there anything you'll be wanting?

JANET. No thank you, Brenda. You finish whatever you're doing and go to bed. (*To* MAURICE.) Why have you got your coat on?

MAURICE. I went to the gate to look for Colin.

JANET. You don't mean to say he didn't turn up.

MAURICE. I'm afraid he didn't.

JANET. But didn't he let you know?

MAURICE. No.

JANET. He didn't even telephone?

MAURICE. No.

JANET. He's *impossible*. Colonel Forbes, do take your coat off. Maurice darling, will you take Colonel Forbes's coat?

COL. FORBES. Thanks. Musn't stay long, though.

JANET. Oh, you're not going without a drink.

(COLONEL FORBES *takes off his coat and* MAURICE *goes out with it to the hall.* BRENDA, *having put more logs on the fire, goes out to kitchen.*)

Mrs. Forbes won't mind you staying a *little* while, I'm sure. What would you like to drink? Whisky? (*To* STELLA.) I hope I'm not offering something we haven't got.

STELLA (*somewhat dazed*). No. No. There is some whisky.

COL. FORBES. That would be very nice. But I hope I'm not going to be the only one.

JANET. No. I'll keep you company. And I expect the others will, too. I'll get some glasses. (*She turns and goes straight towards the cupboard.* STELLA, *starting from down right, has to walk rather fast in an attempt to head her off.*)

STELLA (*loudly*). All right, Janet. I'll get them. You sit down.

(JANET *stops, surprised by the emphasis in* STELLA'S *voice. At the same moment* MAURICE *comes back from the hall and stops between* JANET *and the cupboard. He has left the* COLONEL'S *coat and his own outside.*)

MAURICE. What is it?

JANET. I was going to bring some glasses.

MAURICE. Come and sit down. Stella will look after everything. You must be tired, darling. (*He puts his arm round her and guides her gently to the sofa. There, overjoyed by what she takes for a genuine demonstration of affection on* MAURICE'S *part, she turns and impulsively kisses him.*)

JANET (*softly*). Darling.

MAURICE. Sit down, sit down.

(*She sits on the sofa,* COLONEL FORBES *in an easy chair.* STELLA, *meanwhile, has furtively opened the cupboard and extracted some whisky glasses, with which she now goes to the table where the drinks are.*)

JANET. It's a pity you weren't there, Maurice darling. The conversation at dinner turned on hypnosis. The one person who could have talked about it with authority was missing. However, I did my best to deputize for you.

MAURICE. I'm sure you did very well.

COL. FORBES. Oh, she did. One or two things I don't quite understand, though.

JANET (*with a laugh*). I'm sure there are!

COL. FORBES (*to* MAURICE). For example, I . . . does it, do you *mind* talking about it?

MAURICE (*mechanically*). No, I . . . I don't mind what we talk about.

COL. FORBES. Can you hypnotize *anybody?*

MAURICE. Provided they wish it.

COL. FORBES. And if they don't?

MAURICE. Then you can't. Of course, I'm talking about the first time.

JANET. If you've hypnotized someone often, then you can do it whenever you like and *whether* they wish it or not. Maurice could hypnotize me at this minute . . . even if I didn't want him to.

COL. FORBES. And if they *do* wish it the first time, then it's easy?

MAURICE. It varies.

JANET. Some people are easier than others. Generally speaking the more imagination you have the easier it is to hypnotize you. Aren't I right in saying that an imbecile can't be hypnotized at all?

MAURICE. Quite right.

JANET. I'm glad to say that I was *very* easy.

COL. FORBES. I can well believe it, ma'am!

JANET (*with an ironical bow*). Thank you kindly, sir!

(STELLA *hands whisky and then the soda water to* COLONEL FORBES.)

COL. FORBES. Thank you, thank you.

JANET. The conversation at dinner was about hypnosis and crime, darling.

MAURICE. Oh?

JANET. It was very interesting. There was no one there who really knew a lot about it and most of them knew nothing. But everybody had something to say.

MAURICE. Yes.

JANET. What's the matter, darling? You seem strange and quiet.

MAURICE. No, nothing, nothing. Go on.

JANET. Betty Foster-Wilmott was trying to maintain that you could use hypnosis to persuade someone to commit a crime. For example, a murder. *(STELLA, by this time back at the side-table, drops a whisky glass on to the tray. The others look at her. STELLA, with her back to them, grips the edge of the table and stands for a moment with her head thrown back, struggling to regain her composure.) (Dismissing it.)* Now, of course everyone knows that Betty Foster-Wilmott has the brains of a starved linnet. But you'd be surprised how many people were ready to believe her. *I* said you can persuade people to tell you things that they wouldn't normally tell. And you can make them do things—either during hypnosis or afterwards—that are harmless. But that no one can be made to do something really harmful.

MAURICE. Unless they already had it in them to do it.

JANET. Yes. That's what I said. Oh, I held forth for hours. *(STELLA brings a glass of whisky to JANET.)* Thank you, darling.

STELLA. Soda?

JANET. Please. *(She holds up her glass. STELLA presses too heavily on the siphon and there is an explosion of soda-water all over JANET'S dress.)*

STELLA. Oh God . . . I'm sorry.

JANET. Really, darling, you *could* be a *bit* careful. *(COLONEL FORBES jumps up and produces a handkerchief with which they dab JANET'S dress. MAURICE remains frozen in the middle of the room where he has been all the time.)* What's the matter with you tonight?

STELLA. I don't know, I'm sorry . . . I feel upset, I'm tired, I think.

COL. FORBES. There. No harm done.

JANET *(to STELLA, concerned)*. Darling, it's nothing serious, I hope.

STELLA. No, really. *(She takes the soda siphon back to the side-table.)*

JANET. Are you sure?

STELLA *(over her shoulder)*. Yes, of course.

COL. FORBES *(to MAURICE)*. One more question, if you permit. *(MAURICE makes a gesture of resigned acquiescence.)* I'd like to get this right. If I were harbouring a very harmful desire . . . let us say the desire to do someone in . . . you could, under hypnosis, relieve me of it?

MAURICE. Yes.

COL. FORBES. Could you, under hypnosis, on another occasion, give it back to me?

MAURICE. No doubt.

COL. FORBES. In fact your power for evil would depend very much on mine.

MAURICE. Exactly.

COL. FORBES. Very odd. (*He empties his glass.*)

MAURICE. Exactly.

JANET (*turning to* MAURICE *in surprise*). What on earth's the matter with you tonight?

MAURICE. With me?

JANET. Yes, no, quite right, exactly. You're not usually so tongue-tied on this subject.

MAURICE. I . . . (*He stops.*)

COL. FORBES (*laughing*). Doesn't want to give away the tricks of the trade! That's what it is! Come along now, where's me coat, I must be getting back. Good night, Mrs. Holt, and thank you.

JANET (*as they shake hands*). Good night, Colonel. And thank you for bringing me home.

COL. FORBES. Good night, Miss Holt. I hope you'll feel better in the morning.

MAURICE. I'll come with you.

(*He opens the hall door and shows* COLONEL FORBES *out.*)

JANET. Darling, you're not ill, are you?

STELLA (*protesting*). No, no, good heavens, no!

JANET. You do look a wee bit pale.

STELLA. I'm quite all right, really.

JANET. Stella, darling, I'd like to talk to Maurice for a minute or two when he comes back.

STELLA. You mean alone?

JANET. Would you mind?

STELLA. Well, no, of course not.

JANET (*with a laugh*). Don't look so tragic about it!

STELLA (*protesting*). I wasn't!

JANET. I so seldom get him alone really. He disappears into his little dressing room every night and all day he seems to be busy doing nothing.

STELLA. Darling, if there's something you both want to talk about . . .

JANET. Stella, for heaven's sake don't misunderstand me! I haven't got something to tell him that I don't want you to know about!

STELLA. Well, of *course* not.

JANET. You see, I have to go out, alone, like this, sometimes, don't I? Otherwise I'd never go anywhere. But when I come back I have a sort of odd desire to . . . well, to talk myself back into Maurice's life again. (*Sadly.*) As much in it as I can ever hope to be. Do you see what I mean? I don't know what I'm talking about really. I think I had a little bit too much champagne.

(MAURICE *comes back.*)

MAURICE. Now Janet dear, hadn't you better be going up to bed?

(JANET *recoils from this as from a blow in the face.*)

JANET. Maurice! Oh!

MAURICE. What's the matter?

JANET (*angrily*). Oh, nothing! If that's all you have to say to me I suppose I'd better say good night and go.

MAURICE. I'm tired this evening, Janet darling.

JANET. You're always tired, Maurice! I'm tired, too! Tired of being the third person in this household! I'm *very* tired of that!

STELLA. Darling, wouldn't it be better to talk to Maurice in the morning? I mean . . .

JANET. He'll be asleep in the morning! He'll be tired!

MAURICE. Janet darling, please.

JANET. Janet darling please what? Janet darling please go to bed! (*Almost in tears.*) I don't see why I should be asked to get out of the way the moment I come home . . . I've been out of the way all evening!

(*At a sign from* MAURICE, STELLA *goes out to kitchen, closing the door behind her.* MAURICE *then takes* JANET *in his arms, but she immediately extricates herself and goes to sit on the sofa.*)

No, Maurice, thank you! No affectionate gesture from a sense of duty, if you don't mind.

MAURICE. Aren't you being a little unjust, Janet?

JANET. I made a very silly mistake this evening. But I'll never make it again.

MAURICE. I don't even know what you're talking about.

JANET. When I came in with Colonel Forbes you spoke to me so nicely that I thought . . . well, I thought you meant it. You put your arm round me and said "Come and sit down, darling, you must be tired". I was conscious that I *looked* very nice tonight and I thought perhaps you'd noticed it. I thought you wanted to be alone with me.

MAURICE. Janet dear, there's nothing to be angry or hurt about. You misunderstand me.

JANET (*angrily*). I certainly misunderstood you about that! The whole time Colonel Forbes was here and you were so silent, I was hoping it was because you wanted him to go. And all I got when he *had* gone was "Janet dear, hadn't you better be going up to bed?" (*Rising.*) Oh, it isn't only this evening! You say the same thing every evening! Every evening at a certain moment, "Janet dear, hadn't you better be going up to bed?" (*Growing more and more angry.*) Only usually I'm expecting it! Or at least I'm not expecting anything different! So it doesn't hurt quite so much . . . and I smile and gather up my work and go! Janet dear goes obediently to her room . . . whether she's sleepy or not . . . to lie by herself in that huge, idiotic bed! And I'm tired of that, too! (*Furiously.*) What do you talk about, you and Stella, alone down here, after Janet dear has gone to bed? Every night this week the two of you have crouched over this fire till four in the morning like a couple of old witches, talking, talking, *talking!*

MAURICE. What does it matter what we talk about?

JANET. It matters to me. Am I your wife or not?

MAURICE. Oh, Janet . . .

JANET. I want to know what it is you discuss with Stella that you can't discuss with your wife!

MAURICE. Well, you're not going to know!

JANET. Why not?

MAURICE. Because there's no need!

JANET. Perhaps it's me you discuss!

MAURICE. Till four in the morning? You must think you're very interesting!

JANET. You thought so once! But of course that was when I was ill! You're only interested in people who are ill or mad! The moment you've cured them . . .

MAURICE (*giving way to his anger*). Very well, then, why don't you face it? You *were* more interesting when you were ill! You were very interesting indeed! An unknown quantity! A fascinating problem to be explored and understood! Now all that's over . . . and you're just a wife and I'm just a husband! So face it! And for God's sake have the decency to take the hint!

(*A moment's pause. Then, very calmly—*)

JANET. Very well. I will. I think it only needed you to say that. I'm too mixed up with you emotionally ever to have gone away of my own accord. But I've known I ought to for a long, long time. You don't need anyone but Stella.

(STELLA *comes back.*)

STELLA. Is it really necessary to go on like this half the night?

MAURICE. God in heaven, are *you* starting now?

STELLA. Maurice . . .

MAURICE. If *you* start listening at doors in the middle of the night it will be *too* much!

JANET. Are you suggesting that *I* do that? Because I don't!

MAURICE. I'm afraid you do!

JANET. I think you'd better start analysing *yourself!*

MAURICE (*stung beyond endurance*). You're lying, Janet! Last night . . . or rather at two o'clock this morning . . . you crept out of your room and came half-way down the stairs to lean over the banister and try to hear what we were saying! Didn't you!

JANET (*evasively*). I don't understand what you mean.

MAURICE (*loudly*). Didn't you?

JANET (*caving in*). I may have come out of my room for a minute, but that doesn't mean . . .

MAURICE (*really harshly*). Janet, did you or did you not come down the stairs and try to hear what we were saying?

JANET. I do very much object to you talking as though you were my governess.

MAURICE. Then you shouldn't behave like a child.

JANET. Perhaps if you didn't treat me like one . . . sending me to bed almost as soon as dinner's over . . . I wouldn't!

MAURICE. In any case, if that's the point we've reached . . . lies and deceit and listening on stairways . . . perhaps you're right. We'd better not go on. Now go to bed! And tonight . . . now that you know that we know . . . perhaps you won't spy on us!

(JANET *goes and picks up her coat and bag. Then she turns to him again.*)

JANET. There's one thing I think you should ask yourself, Maurice. When someone whose confidence you once possessed becomes deceitful I think you should ask yourself whether perhaps it isn't . . . to some *extent* . . . your fault.

(JANET *turns and goes wretchedly towards the hall door. Suddenly, however, there is a violent knocking on the glass of the french*

H.B.L.—D

windows. JANET *stops. They all look towards the windows and then*
at each other. The knocking is repeated and IRIS's *voice is heard, off.)*
IRIS (*off*). Janet! Maurice!
> (*More knocking.* MAURICE *goes and draws the curtains.* IRIS *and*
> MR. HOWARD *are standing outside.* MAURICE *opens and they come in.*
> *It is quite dark again now in the garden.*
>   IRIS *looks ghastly—very white and strained. She has a piece of*
> *sticking plaster across her temple. She speaks hysterically.*)
We've been ringing the front door bell for hours!
MAURICE. I'm sorry.
IRIS (*angrily*). Didn't you hear?
MAURICE. If we'd heard we'd have answered!
STELLA. I'm afraid Brenda's gone to bed. We were all in here.
JANET. Whatever's the matter, Iris?
IRIS. Where's Colin? Has he been here?
MAURICE. No. He was supposed to, but he didn't turn up.
IRIS. I know.
MAURICE. If you know why are you asking? And incidentally *how* did
    you know?
IRIS. This gentleman arrived at the house. I was out. He phoned you.
HOWARD. I'd better introduce myself.
IRIS. I'm sorry. This is Mr. Howard.
MAURICE }
STELLA   } (*together*). How d'you do?
HOWARD. How d'you do?
JANET. We met this morning.
HOWARD. Yes.
IRIS. Mr. Howard is a detective, Maurice. I'd better tell you that I'm
    under arrest.
JANET. Iris!
MAURICE. What are you talking about? (*To* HOWARD.) Is this true?
HOWARD. No. No one is under arrest yet.
IRIS. I shall be very soon. I've done it, Janet . . . Maurice . . .
    Stella. I've killed him. (*She puts her face into her hands.* JANET *goes to*
    her.)
JANET. Iris . . . darling . . . (*She takes* IRIS's *hands away from her face.*)
IRIS. I've killed Colin, Janet.
JANET (*very alarmed*). Iris! Come . . . darling . . . sit down.
>   (*She leads her to the sofa.* IRIS *sinks on to it, white and trembling,*
> *and puts her hand over her face again.* JANET *kneels in front of her.*)

Now, tell us exactly what you mean . . . don't be frightened, darling . . . we shall look after you. (*Over her shoulder, to* MAURICE.) Get some brandy, quickly.

(MAURICE *goes to the table where the drinks are, picks up a bottle of brandy and pours some into a glass.*)

Darling, what's happened to your head?

IRIS. He did it.

JANET. He hit you?

IRIS. He knocked me down. I fell against the table.

JANET (*softly*). Oh, my God. (*Turning* IRIS's *head very slightly with her fingers.*) You've been cut here, too . . . my poor darling.

(IRIS *shakes her head and relapses into tears, feeling in her pockets for a handkerchief.* JANET *produces one.* MAURICE *brings the glass of brandy.*)

MAURICE. Don't try to talk for a minute, Iris. Drink this first.

(JANET *takes the glass and holds it to* IRIS's *mouth. During the following lines* IRIS *dries her eyes and drinks the brandy.* HOWARD *lights a cigarette.*)

(*To* HOWARD.) How much do you know about this? What happened?

HOWARD. I'm not certain yet.

MAURICE. How did you get into it?

HOWARD. Oh, that's simple. I've been looking for your brother for the last three days. I was never able to find him at his office. This morning I came out here . . . your wife told me where the house was . . . but I missed him.

MAURICE. May I ask what you want him for?

HOWARD. Yes. I want to speak to him in connection with the falsification of the accounts of a company of which he's the managing director.

MAURICE. What company?

HOWARD. The Brocklebank Saw Mills.

MAURICE. I know quite a lot about that. My sister and I are part owners of it.

HOWARD. I'm sorry to hear it.

STELLA. Why? What's happened?

HOWARD. Did either of you know that certain cheques have been forged in connection with that company?

MAURICE. Good God, no.

HOWARD (*to* STELLA). Did you?

STELLA. Well, of course not.

HOWARD (*examining the end of his cigarette*). Well, it is so.
> (*A moment's pause.*)
> I went back to your brother's house again this evening . . . hoping to catch him before he left to come here.

MAURICE (*warmly*). I've told you he didn't come!

HOWARD. Mrs. Holt was out. I phoned from the house. Spoke to you, I think, didn't I? I thought perhaps I'd get a word with him here. You told me he hadn't arrived. I didn't believe it at the moment. However, I waited in case he came back. Then Mrs. Holt came in. And she told me something rather sensational.

IRIS. I told you what I'd done, that's all. Why don't you arrest me?

HOWARD. Perhaps you'll tell your brother-in-law what you told me.
> (*Fortified by the brandy,* IRIS *rises.*)

IRIS. I put some morphine into his whisky. That's what I did.

JANET. Iris!

MAURICE. Where did you get morphine from?

JANET (*angrily*). She got it from Nurse Thomson who had no right at all to let her have it!

HOWARD. By the way, Nurse Thomson should be with us at any minute. We telephoned and asked her to meet us here. Do you mind if we leave a door open so that we hear the bell?
> (JANET *goes and opens the hall door.*)
> If what Mrs. Holt says is true, Nurse Thomson will be an important witness. And indeed an accessory before the fact.

IRIS (*furiously*). But of course it's true! (*To the others.*) Mr. Howard doesn't seem to believe me! But he will!

HOWARD. I'm sorry, Mrs. Holt, but I can't arrest you for murdering your husband until I know he's dead.

MAURICE (*severely*). Iris, will you please tell me exactly what happened.

IRIS (*distraught*). Yes. That's what I came here for! (*After a moment, very quietly.*) We had a scene. The worst we've ever had. Of course about money . . . he wanted me to try to get money for him from my father which I can't do. He lost his temper. We both did. He said I'd have to clear out, for good, and without a penny. Then he started to knock me about. After I fell and did this—(*Touching her forehead.*)—he kicked me. Then he went out of the room and I got up. I was crying and my head was bleeding. I felt I couldn't stand it any more. I intended to take the morphine. I went and got it. Then I suddenly saw his whisky flask. It was too easy and too

tempting. I was boiling over with hatred. I put the morphine into
the whisky . . . the whole lot.

       (A moment's pause.)

JANET *(softly)*. My God.

IRIS *(her voice beginning to tremble)*. I went out of the house. I walked
about. I didn't know where I was going. Then I found myself in
the church. I was alone. *(Beginning to cry.)* I stayed there a long time.
And I prayed.

    (A moment's pause. HOWARD *puts out his cigarette.)*

Then I went home intending to call the police. And I found Mr.
Howard there. *(Softly.)* That's all. *(She cries softly into her hand-*
kerchief. JANET *makes her sit down. The others stare at her for a moment.)*

JANET. Come, darling, don't cry.

STELLA. What exactly do you mean when you say whisky flask, Iris?
You mean the little silver one he carries with him?

IRIS *(blowing her nose)*. Yes.

JANET *(suddenly)*. But where is he? What are we to do? We must find
him. He may not have touched it yet! There may be time still!
(Kneeling to IRIS *again.)* Iris darling, think. Try to think hard. Did
he say anything at all at any moment of the day that might give us
a clue as to where he is?

    *(*IRIS *shakes her head. The door bell is heard.)*

(Rising.) Wait a minute. I'll go.

    *(*JANET *goes out to hall.* HOWARD *produces a cigarette case and*
offers it to IRIS, *who shakes her head. He offers it then to* STELLA.)*

STELLA. No, thank you.

HOWARD. Please.

STELLA. Thank you. I don't.

    (He offers it to MAURICE.)*

MAURICE. Nor do I. Thank you.

    *(*HOWARD *lights his cigarette as* JANET *comes back, accompanying*
NURSE THOMSON. NURSE THOMSON *is a plump, healthy looking*
woman in the thirties, with eyeglasses and gold hair. She is in uniform
and carries a little leather bag. She is brisk and full of common sense.)

NURSE *(brightly)*. Good evening all! What can I do for you?

MAURICE⎫
      (together). Good evening, Nurse.
STELLA ⎭

IRIS *(softly)*. Hello, dear.

NURSE *(in surprise)*. Mrs. Holt! What's wrong?

MAURICE. Nurse, this is Mr. Howard.

HOWARD⎱ (*together*). How d'you do?
NURSE ⎰

MAURICE. He's from the police. He wants to ask you some questions.

NURSE (*alarmed*). What's happened?

JANET. Well, we don't know that anything's happened yet, Nurse. The fact is . . .

MAURICE. Janet dear, you'd better let Mr. Howard do the talking, don't you think?

JANET (*meekly*). I'm sorry, darling.

HOWARD. You're the District Nurse, eh?

NURSE. Yes.

HOWARD. I'd better give you the customary warning.

NURSE. Anything I say may be used in evidence. Yes, all right, get on with it.

HOWARD. In my own time, Nurse, in my own time.

NURSE. There's no need to be long-winded about it. What's happened?

HOWARD. You know Mr. Colin Holt?

NURSE (*sarcastically*). Well, of course I know him. I know everybody.

HOWARD. There seems to be a possibility that he's been murdered, Nurse.

NURSE. I'm not at all surprised. By whom?

HOWARD. By Mrs. Holt.

NURSE. Nonsense.

HOWARD (*patiently*). Nurse, I'm not asking your opinion as to what is probable or otherwise. I just want you to give me some facts.

NURSE. All right. What facts?

HOWARD. You've been visiting Mrs. Holt every day to give her injections.

NURSE. Yes.

HOWARD. She was allowed by the doctor at one time to have small quantities of morphine.

NURSE. Yes.

HOWARD. Given to her by you, a little at a time.

NURSE. Yes.

HOWARD. Until about six months ago when the doctor said she wasn't to have any more.

NURSE. Since you seem to know it all I don't know what you're asking me.

HOWARD. I'm asking you to confirm what Mrs. Holt has told me.
NURSE. Well. Go on.
HOWARD. Some weeks ago she began to ask for morphine again.
NURSE. Yes.
HOWARD. The doctor still refused?
NURSE. Yes.
HOWARD. Did she then ask you to steal some for her?
NURSE (*after a second*). She asked me to procure some for her.
    (HOWARD *dismisses the distinction with a little wave of his cigarette.
    Then, a trifle sarcastically*—)
HOWARD. You were to "procure" her a small quantity whenever you could?
NURSE. Yes.
HOWARD. And, in fact, every day, for a fortnight or more, you did?
NURSE. Yes.
HOWARD. You had no right to do that.
NURSE. That's my business.
HOWARD. Miss Thomson, I do represent the police, you know.
NURSE. From the cross examination you might be Counsel for the Prosecution. However, that doesn't worry me. I've nothing on my conscience. It wasn't morphine in those capsules. It was castor sugar.
    (IRIS *rises.*)
MAURICE (*blankly*). Castor sugar? What are you talking about?
HOWARD. Is this true?
JANET (*with relief*). Nurse!
NURSE (*to* IRIS). I'm sorry, dear. But I was *afraid* you were collecting it. I didn't know you intended it for *Mr.* Holt. I thought you intended it for yourself. So I bought the capsules empty, from the chemist, and I filled them with castor sugar.
    (IRIS *throws herself, sobbing with relief, into* NURSE THOMSON'S *arms.*)
There, there, now. Don't worry any more, dear. (*To* JANET.) Mrs. Holt, have you any brandy?
    (JANET *takes the glass that* IRIS *used before and puts more brandy into it. During the following lines she ministers to* IRIS.)
HOWARD (*to* MAURICE). Well, that rather alters the look of things.
MAURICE. I'm afraid you've had quite a lot of trouble for nothing, Mr. Howard.
HOWARD. Yes. Perhaps.
MAURICE. I don't see any perhaps about it.

HOWARD. There's still the other little matter to go into—isn't there?
. . . when your brother turns up.

MAURICE. Is that so urgent?

HOWARD. It hasn't become any less urgent because he's still alive.

MAURICE. I only thought it seems a little late. You'll miss the last train
back to Town.

HOWARD. Yes. Pity.

MAURICE. In any case he won't come here at this hour.

HOWARD. I'll take Mrs. Holt back home. He may be there by now.

MAURICE. Yes. Oh yes. Yes. You'd better go with them, Janet, and
look after Iris.

JANET. Well of course. Come along, darling, we'll take you home.
All right now?

IRIS. I'm all right.

JANET. There's just one thing. I think we must none of us say anything
about this. You do see what I mean, Mr. Howard.

HOWARD. When he turns up . . . Mr. Holt will have other things to
think about.

JANET. I'll get my coat. (*She goes out to the hall.* IRIS, *still very shaky,
puts away her handkerchief and goes to* MAURICE.)

IRIS (*kissing him*). I'm sorry, Maurice dear . . . disturbing your peaceful
evening. (*She turns to* STELLA. *Kissing her.*) You forgive me?

STELLA (*nervously*). Of course, dear, of course. Get to bed now.

    (JANET *comes back putting on a big coat.*)

JANET. We'll pick up a taxi at the station.

IRIS. Thank you. I'd like some air.

NURSE (*to* JANET). I think I'll come with you. I'll give her an injection.
(*Smiling at* IRIS.) Make her go to sleep, shall we? Well, good night,
all. (*To* IRIS.) Come along, dear.

MAURICE ⎱
STELLA ⎰ (*together*). Good night.

    (NURSE THOMSON *puts an arm round* IRIS *and takes her out by
the hall door.*)

HOWARD. Good night. (*Shakes hands with* STELLA *and with* MAURICE.)

MAURICE. Good night, Mr. Howard.

JANET (*putting on her gloves*). I shan't be long. We'll put her to bed.
She'll be all right. Mr. Howard, would you wait for me with the
others for just one second? There's something I want to say to my
husband.

HOWARD. Of course.

(He goes out. JANET *goes to* MAURICE. *She is suddenly transformed into the humble, dependent* JANET *of Act One.)*

JANET. I'm sorry I spoke like that, darling.

MAURICE *(a shade impatiently)*. Oh, Janet, that's all right.

JANET *(putting her arms round him)*. It was silly. I didn't mean it. I think I'd had too much champagne. Please say you forgive me, darling. *(Nestling against him.)* You may have gone to bed when I get back.

MAURICE *(kissing her)*. There.

JANET *(softly)*. Thank you. What possessed me suddenly to behave like that I can't imagine. You must admit it isn't like me.

MAURICE. Subconscious perhaps.

JANET *(to* STELLA*)*. Good night, Stella.

STELLA. Good night, darling.

(The two women kiss. Then JANET *goes to the hall door. There she turns.)*

JANET *(to* MAURICE*)*. If it was my subconscious then it's all *your* fault! I consider my subconscious to be *your* affair!

(She smiles and goes out, closing the door. A moment's pause. Then—)

STELLA. What do we do?

*(*MAURICE *holds up his hand. Then he goes to the hall door, opens it and listens. The front door is heard to slam.* MAURICE *turns to* STELLA.*)*

MAURICE. We carry on as though nothing had happened. It's the only thing we can do.

He goes and puts the main lights out as—

THE CURTAIN FALLS.

ACT THREE

SCENE I

The scene is the same. The time is the afternoon of the following day. When the curtain rises, JANET, MAURICE *and* STELLA *are present. They are drinking tea.*
  Outside it is dusk. There is already at least one lamp lighted in the room.

STELLA. I wish you'd try to get some sleep, Janet. You must be worn out.

JANET. Oh, I'm all right. It's Iris I'm worried about. I'll go over again after tea.

STELLA. As a matter of curiosity, why didn't Iris go to bed last night, when you got her home? Surely that was the idea.

JANET. She wouldn't.

STELLA. I thought Nurse Thomson was going to give her something to make her sleep.

JANET. She did. But it seemed to have no effect at all.

STELLA. I suppose she was too worked up.

JANET. I think she was afraid that when Colin came in one of us would say something. Then of course . . . as the hours went by and he didn't come at all . . . she became more and more wide awake and . . . well, apprehensive. And of course since six o'clock this morning the place has been full of people asking questions.

STELLA (*after a moment*). Was it she who thought of . . . the lake?

JANET. No. I did.

  (*A pause. Then* MAURICE, *looking into his tea cup and stirring it, speaks very casually.*)

MAURICE. The police appear to think it happened on the way here.

JANET. Well, yes. It's rather obvious, isn't it?

MAURICE. I suppose it is.

JANET. I'm surprised he didn't come by the road all the same. It was a very dark night. Everyone knew it was thawing. And we'd warned him.

MAURICE (*softly*). Colin was always obstinate.

(*A pause.*)

JANET. Rather an ironical coincidence, wasn't it?

(MAURICE *and* STELLA *both turn their heads to her.*)

I mean that half an hour after Iris's pathetic attempt . . . Fate proved it to have been unnecessary. If only for some reason she'd had to postpone it until today she could have told herself that of course she'd never have actually done it. But now she has to live the rest of her life facing the fact that she *did*. It was only Nurse Thomson's precautions that made her fail. Iris has proved herself a murderess.

STELLA (*rising suddenly*). I shouldn't brood on that if I were you. You'll become morbid.

MAURICE. I think there are more important problems, certainly. For example, her financial situation.

STELLA. You don't know whether he's made a will?

MAURICE. I've no idea. Indeed, has he anything to leave?

STELLA. We can hardly go into that today. But presumably we're free now to sell the Brocklebank Mills.

MAURICE. Yes. Minus what there was in the bank, that's ours.

STELLA. Did he get away with very much?

MAURICE. Can't have done. The account contained only a few hundred pounds. Luckily.

JANET. Don't you think we ought at least to wait until he's buried before going into all the horrible things he did?

MAURICE. I see no point in sentimentalizing death. I never have. Colin gave us hell the whole of the time he was alive. My attitude towards him hasn't changed because he's dead. Why should I pretend it has? And why wait until he's buried before feeling we can say what we think? He's dead. We hated him. And we're glad. Before, during and after the funeral.

(*The telephone rings.* MAURICE *gets up and goes to answer it.*)

Yes? . . . Speaking. (*Long pause.*) What, now? I suppose so, if it's necessary. But why? Anything special? (*Another pause.*) Well, I suppose we must, mustn't we? In twenty minutes . . . we'll walk round. Thank you. (*He replaces the receiver. To* STELLA.) Inspector Edwards. Busy little man, Inspector Edwards. He wants us to go back again.

JANET. All of us?

MAURICE. No. Just Stella and me.

STELLA. Why doesn't he come here? And what does he want now, anyway?

MAURICE. He says he'd like to ask us a few more questions. Inspector Edwards is taking himself *very* seriously. By nine o'clock this morning he'd already filled two notebooks with spelling mistakes. Well, we'll have to go, I suppose. I'll get my coat. (*He goes out to hall. STELLA puts her tea cup on the tray. Then she collects MAURICE's and does the same with that.*)

JANET. Don't bother about those. I'll get Brenda.

(*She goes and rings the bell by the fireplace. MAURICE comes back, putting on his coat. He remains in the doorway. STELLA passes him and goes out.*)

MAURICE. I don't suppose we shall be long.

JANET. Tell Iris I'll come and see her later.

MAURICE. Very well.

JANET. Darling, I'm sorry if what I said just now seemed like a criticism.

MAURICE (*wearily*). Oh Janet, for God's sake stop apologizing all the time!

(*BRENDA has just entered from the kitchen.*)

BRENDA. Were you wanting something, ma'am?

JANET. Oh. Yes. Thank you, Brenda. The tea things.

MAURICE. See you later. (*He goes out to the hall, closing the door.*)

(*BRENDA picks up the tea tray.*)

BRENDA. I think I'll go down to the village, ma'am. I've one or two things I'm wanting. Can I bring you anything?

JANET. No, Brenda, thank you.

BRENDA (*putting the tray down again*). Oh, by the way, I was nearly forgetting! Now isn't that a queer thing. Look what I found in the garden! A cigarette lighter. Imagine that! (*She takes it from the pocket of her apron and gives it to JANET.*)

JANET. How strange. I wonder whose it . . . (*She gasps.*) But it's Mr. Colin's!

BRENDA. That's what I thought by the initials.

JANET. But how . . . where was it?

BRENDA. Why, just on the path there . . . by the wood shed.

JANET (*baffled*). On the path by the wood shed?

BRENDA. In the snow, at the side.

(*JANET stares at the little gold lighter in amazement.*)

Poor man. He'll not be missing it. He must have let it fall there

yesterday morning. Little did he think that when it was found he'd
not be needing it. Still working too, it is. It makes you think.

JANET (*absently*). What? Oh yes.

(HOWARD *appears at the french windows and taps on the glass.*)

Oh. There's Mr. Howard. All right, Brenda. I'll let him in.

BRENDA. You're very kind, ma'am.

(*She goes out to the kitchen with the tray while* JANET *opens the
french windows for* HOWARD.)

HOWARD. Good evening.

JANET. My husband's just gone out. You met him, I suppose?

HOWARD. No. I expect they've gone by the road.

JANET. I should say so. But didn't you come that way?

HOWARD. No. I came across the lake.

JANET (*horrified*). You didn't! You walked across the ice . . . after
what happened last night?

(*A long pause.* HOWARD *looks around with his queer smile.
Then—*)

HOWARD. I examined the ice very carefully this morning . . . when
your brother-in-law had been taken away. I even jumped up and
down on it. It didn't break.

JANET. Is it necessary to take risks like that?

HOWARD. In my profession . . . yes.

JANET. Will you sit down and wait?

HOWARD. No, thank you. But I'd like a cigarette. I seem to have
run out.

(JANET *goes to the table, picks up the cigarette box and hands it to
him. He takes one and examines it.*)

You're the only one in the house who smokes?

JANET. I am.

HOWARD. You always smoke these?

JANET. Yes. Why?

HOWARD. Oh, I just wondered.

JANET. How did you know I was the only one who smoked?

HOWARD. I offered a cigarette to your husband and his sister last night.
She said, "Thank you, I don't" . . . and he said, "Nor do I"

JANET (*mystified*). Is this of any importance?

HOWARD. *Anything* can be important in these cases, you know.

JANET. But is there a case?

HOWARD (*lighting a cigarette*). Oh yes

JANET. But isn't it obvious that the ice gave way and he was drowned?
(There is a pause.)

HOWARD. Sit down, Mrs. Holt. And I'll tell you something.

(JANET mechanically obeys, staring at him in mystification.)

Since breakfast time this morning quite a lot has happened. Your brother-in-law was taken from the lake at six o'clock. A lot of people have been drowned in the last few days in England by falling through the ice. If I hadn't happened to be here . . . if we hadn't had that curious interlude with Mr. Holt's wife last night . . . no doubt this would have passed for just another accident. As it was, however, I thought it would be interesting to have an autopsy. Which was performed later in the morning. By two o'clock it was over and I was given the result. Your brother-in-law was dead when he entered the water.

(JANET rises.)

JANET (under her breath). No!

HOWARD. Also . . . he had been poisoned.

JANET (staggered). But I . . . you mean . . . Nurse Thomson . . .

HOWARD. That's the theory the police are working on.

JANET. Does Mrs. Holt know this?

HOWARD. Indeed she does. She was arrested an hour ago.

JANET. My God! Poor Iris.

HOWARD. Nurse Thomson will also have been arrested by now.

(JANET puts her face into her hands.)

(Softly.) Yes. It's very serious.

JANET. We must tell my husband! I must telephone to him!

HOWARD. Wait! Don't do that! It was I who arranged for him and his sister to be sent for. So that I could talk to you.

JANET. Why to me?

HOWARD. Because . . . of the four people who live in this house . . . two have alibis for their movements last night. You and your maid.

(A pause.)

JANET (stupefied). Are you suggesting . . .? (She stops.)

HOWARD. I'm not suggesting it yet, no.

JANET. Will you tell me what you mean?

HOWARD (after a moment). Do you think it possible that Mr. Colin Holt did come here to dinner last night?

JANET. Good heavens, no! Of course not!

HOWARD. I asked your maid a few questions this morning· Very casually. I didn't want to excite her.

JANET. What did you ask her?

HOWARD. I wondered if she'd noticed anything to suggest that he'd been here. I don't think she did. Did you?

JANET. No.

HOWARD. I did.

JANET (*breathlessly*). What?

HOWARD (*picking up the cigarette box*). Have you any cigarettes apart from these?

JANET. I think I have a packet in my bag.

HOWARD. Same brand?

JANET. Yes.

HOWARD. Do you ever smoke cigarettes with filter tips?

JANET. No.

HOWARD (*putting the box down again*). There was a filter-tipped cigarette in this ash tray last night. Unsmoked.

JANET. Are you sure?

HOWARD. Positive.

JANET. But, but, but . . . where could it have come from?

HOWARD. Mr. Colin Holt's cigarette case contained others of the same brand. It *might* have come from there.

JANET (*softly*). Good God.

HOWARD. However, that isn't quite enough to prove that he was here last night. He might have left it here yesterday morning. Might have dropped it.

JANET. No, Mr. Howard. He must have been here last night.

(JANET *produces from the pocket of her skirt the cigarette lighter and holds it out on the flat of her hand.*)

That's his.

HOWARD (*taking it*). Where did this come from?

JANET. Brenda found it, an hour or two ago, on the path leading to the lake.

HOWARD. Quite interesting.

JANET. And that can't have been dropped yesterday morning.

HOWARD. Why not?

JANET (*quickly*). Because yesterday morning he used it in here. He lighted a cigarette for me with it. And when he left . . . with that in his pocket . . . he went by the front garden, on his way to Town

HOWARD. Thank you, Mrs. Holt. You're being a great help.

JANET. I'm afraid if there were any finger-prints Brenda and I . . .

HOWARD. Alas, there wouldn't have been. (*Disgusted.*) Look at that! Sheer vandalistic destruction of surface. Sometimes I think I'll found a royal society for the abolition of engine turning. (*He puts the lighter into his pocket.*)

JANET. Mr. Howard . . . even if he did come here last night . . . it was still Iris who put the morphine into his . . .

HOWARD. Forget about the morphine, Mrs. Holt. The body contained **no morphine at all. It contained a large quantity of hyoscine.** Probably administered in coffee, by the way—not whisky.

JANET. Then why has Inspector Edwards arrested his wife?

HOWARD. Forget about Inspector Edwards, Mrs. Holt. He's going on the assumption that Nurse Thomson was lying. So long as Mr. Holt's whisky flask contains something more interesting than sugar he'll be happy. But it will contain sugar . . . and nothing else.

JANET. You seem very sure.

HOWARD. I don't think Nurse Thomson was lying. Anyway, here it is. (*He takes from his pocket a small hip-flask of glass and silver.*) It will be analysed this evening. But in any case it's of little interest. Do you see why? (*He hands it to her. She takes it very circumspectly.*) It's all right. You can handle it. **We've taken the finger-prints. His wife's . . . naturally.**

JANET (*suddenly*). Good heavens! Of course it's of no interest! It's full!

HOWARD. You're doing very well, Mrs. Holt. Yes, it's full. He didn't even take it out with him.

JANET (*handing it back*). Where was it?

HOWARD. In a cupboard in his dressing room. (*He puts it back into his pocket.*)

(*A moment's pause.*)

JANET. Mr. Howard . . . I feel frightened.

HOWARD. Now don't say that.

JANET. Maurice and Stella! It isn't *possible!*

HOWARD. We must assume it's possible.

JANET. No, no, no! I don't believe it! I *won't* believe it!

HOWARD. Keep calm, Mrs. Holt. You've got to help me.

JANET. Oh, my God, there's nothing *I* can do! If this is true . . .

HOWARD (*firmly*). Mrs. Holt!

JANET. I'm sorry, I'm sorry . . . it's *too* awful.

HOWARD. Now listen . . . carefully . . . we've no time to lose.

JANET. Yes, I'm listening.

HOWARD. Your husband and his sister know something. You're going to find out what it is.

JANET. Yes, yes. There may be some simple explanation . . . I'll question them as soon as they come in.

HOWARD. No!

JANET. But I *must!* I must know what's happened!

HOWARD. If you ask . . . I'm afraid you won't find out.

JANET. Are you suggesting that my husband would tell me a lie?

HOWARD (*tactfully*). Mightn't he, Mrs. Holt? If only to protect you from something?

JANET (*softly*). Yes. I'm afraid it's true. I'm always being protected and kept in the dark.

HOWARD. Whereas . . . if you simply observe . . . ?

JANET. Observe?

(HOWARD *takes the cigarette lighter from his pocket. During the following lines she tries to protest but he raises his voice and she subsides.*)

HOWARD. Mrs. Holt, you will arrange for this to be found once more. By your husband. In your presence. Though you won't appear to notice. If he has nothing on his conscience he'll say, "Good heavens! Look at this! Colin's lighter!"

JANET. Where . . . where must I hide it?

HOWARD. I think . . . somewhere in this room. (*He hands it to her. She takes it as though it were a piece of dynamite.*)

JANET (*suddenly*). Wouldn't it be better if I spoke to him, Mr. Howard? I mean . . .

HOWARD (*sharply*). Mrs. Holt! Whatever happens . . . *whatever* happens . . . your husband and his sister mustn't know what you suspect. They mustn't know that you've seen me. Whatever they tell you when they come back . . . receive it as news . . . just as though I hadn't been here at all. One other thing. Tell your maid on no account to mention what she found to either of them.

JANET. She's out.

HOWARD. Then the moment she comes back. (*He takes out a notebook and pencil.*) I'm going to give you a telephone number. (*Writing.*) This is where I shall be between eight and nine this evening. (*He tears out the page and gives it to JANET.*) If you feel yourself to be in the slightest . . . danger . . . call me. (*Looking at his watch.*) Now I must go. (*He holds out his hand. JANET puts the piece of paper into her pocket.*) Keep cool. (*They shake hands. He goes to the french windows.*)

H.B.L.—E

JANET (*nervously*). Mr. Howard! When, when, when will you come back?

HOWARD. In the morning. I'll arrange for them to be called away again. (*He steps outside and then turns to her again.*) Now remember. You haven't seen me. You know nothing.

JANET. Mr. Howard, I can't do this. It's too horrible.

(HOWARD *looks at her for a second then closes the french windows, turns up his collar and goes. Outside it is nearly dark.*

Left alone, JANET *looks at the cigarette lighter in her hand. Then she puts it down on the table, goes to the french windows and closes the curtains. When she has done this she comes slowly back to centre looking around her, wondering where to place the lighter. She picks it up and puts it under the cushion of the sofa. Then, after a moment's reflection, she decides against this and takes it out again. Suddenly she stops and listens. She goes to the hall door, opens it softly and then quickly closes it and comes back to centre. She puts the lighter just under a corner of the sofa at the front. She then goes to the table, takes a cigarette and lights it. The match trembles in her fingers to such a degree that she has great difficulty.*

MAURICE *comes in from the hall. He is extremely agitated.*)

MAURICE. Janet, Iris has been arrested.

JANET (*with a great effort*). Iris?

MAURICE. Yes. At lunch-time. Nurse Thomson too.

JANET. But . . . I don't understand.

MAURICE. There's been an autopsy. Colin *was* poisoned.

JANET. My God.

(*A pause.* MAURICE *walks up and down in great agitation.* JANET *watches him.*)

Who told you this? Mr. Howard?

MAURICE. No. Inspector Edwards told us. Mr. Howard wasn't there. He'd left for London.

JANET. What do they think?

MAURICE. They think Nurse Thomson was lying.

JANET. Do you?

MAURICE. Well, of course! What other explanation could there be? (*He stands and looks at her.*)

JANET. I . . . I don't know.

MAURICE (*walking up and down again*). When she was questioned here last night she obviously told the first lie that came into her head.

JANET. She was very cool, don't you think?

MAURICE. She's a clever woman.

JANET (*looking at her cigarette*). So it was morphine after all. *Not* castor sugar.

MAURICE. Funnily enough it wasn't morphine.

JANET. Really? What was it?

MAURICE. It was hyoscine.

JANET. Then why did Iris think she was collecting morphine? Isn't that rather strange?

MAURICE (*vehemently*). Why is it strange? She thought she was receiving morphine! In fact it was hyoscine. Surely that's for Nurse Thomson to explain!

JANET. You sound very angry.

MAURICE. I'm not angry. I'm upset.

(*A pause.*)

JANET. Where's Stella?

MAURICE. She'll be here in a minute. She went to get the evening paper. Apparently there's something in it.

(*Another pause.*)

JANET. So you believe that Iris is guilty?

MAURICE. She told us so herself, didn't she?

JANET. But how did he get into the lake?

MAURICE. No doubt she and Nurse Thomson carried him there.

JANET. And smashed a hole in the ice and put him in?

MAURICE. It wouldn't be impossible.

JANET. Iris is not very strong.

MAURICE. Nurse Thomson is.

JANET. But why didn't Iris confess to that part of it, too? There was no reason not to . . . after telling us the rest.

MAURICE. How do *I* know?

JANET (*softly*). I was just wondering what . . . what your theory was, (MAURICE *walks up and down again. Then he sees the lighter. He stops dead. He has his back to* JANET *and she sees him make the discovery. She immediately turns away and walks slowly towards the fireplace.* MAURICE, *after glancing at her retreating back, quickly bends down and picks up the lighter. When she reaches the fireplace* JANET *flicks the ash from her cigarette into the fire. Then she turns to* MAURICE *again. He is now facing her, his hands at his side.* JANET, *with a great effort, speaks casually.*) Did they find . . . the whisky flask?

MAURICE. Yes.

JANET. And it contained some of this . . . this stuff?
MAURICE. I've no idea.

(*A pause.*)

JANET. What is the next step?
MAURICE. The inquest . . . tomorrow.
JANET. Shall we have to go to it?
MAURICE. No doubt.
JANET. Not that we can tell them anything, can we?
MAURICE. Nothing at all. Well . . . I think I'll go up to my room for a while.
JANET (*softly*). Yes.
MAURICE. *You* don't know of anything that could give us any clue as to what exactly happened?
JANET. Me? No. Why?
MAURICE. I just wondered. (*He walks across the room and runs his finger along a table. Then he looks at it.*) Did Brenda not do this room this morning?
JANET. No. There was rather too much . . . going on. I'm sorry.
MAURICE. It's of no importance.

(STELLA *enters from hall. She is wearing a coat, but no hat, and carries a folded newspaper.*)

STELLA. I got the paper. There's nothing much. (*Undoing her coat.*) I met Brenda in the village. She tells me she found Colin's cigarette lighter in the garden.

(*Both* MAURICE *and* JANET *are knocked nearly senseless by this remark. There is a long pause.* JANET *tries to speak but seems literally unable to do so.* MAURICE *is the first to recover.*)

MAURICE (*to* STELLA). What did she say?
JANET. Maurice . . .

(*He holds up a hand and she stops.*)

STELLA. She simply said she'd found it and given it to Janet.
JANET (*in agony*). Maurice . . .
MAURICE. Wait, Janet! (*To* STELLA.) Where did she find it?
STELLA (*astonished*). Didn't you know . . . about this?
MAURICE. No.
STELLA (*looking at* JANET). I thought Janet would have told you.
MAURICE. You would have thought so, yes.

(*They look at* JANET. *She is in great distress. She sinks on to the sofa.*)

STELLA (*puzzled*). What has happened?

> (MAURICE *takes the cigarette lighter from his pocket and turns it round in his fingers. All through the following scene* JANET *speaks very softly, so frightened that she can hardly speak at all.*)

MAURICE. Here it is. It's been found twice, Stella.

STELLA. Twice?

MAURICE. Once in the garden apparently . . . by Brenda. And once in here . . . a minute ago . . . by me. (*After a moment.*) What *was* this, Janet? A trap?

JANET. Why did you pretend?

MAURICE. Pretend?

JANET. That you hadn't found it. You picked it up and slipped it into your pocket and said, "I think I'll go to my room".

MAURICE. I'm afraid I didn't attach any importance to it, Janet.

JANET. Colin's lighter? Found here? Today? Not important?

MAURICE. Is it? I imagine he dropped it here yesterday morning.

JANET. No.

MAURICE. Why not?

JANET. Maurice . . . he was here last night, wasn't he?

MAURICE. What makes you think that?

JANET. He was using that lighter here yesterday morning. He left by the front, with Iris. Brenda found it at the back . . . half-way down to the lake.

MAURICE. Well, well. And she gave it to you and you placed it here for me to find.

JANET (*a whisper*). Yes.

> (*He sits beside her.* STELLA *crosses behind the sofa and comes to stand at the end of it, looking down at* JANET'S *back.*)

MAURICE. Your own idea?

JANET. Yes.

MAURICE. Why didn't you tell Brenda to keep her mouth shut?

JANET. I . . . I didn't think . . . think of it till after she'd gone out.

MAURICE. Not very clever—are you?—in the *rôle* of a sleuth!

JANET. I didn't . . . I . . .

MAURICE. Well?

JANET (*very softly*). What have you done?

STELLA. My dear, your imagination seems to be running away with you.

> (JANET *tries to rise, but* MAURICE *pulls her down on to the sofa again.*)

MAURICE. Come, Janet. Let's hear about it. This . . . finding of this thing . . . made you think that Stella and I know something?

JANET. You do . . . don't you? I think you do.

MAURICE. Well now, if you think that . . .

JANET. Oh my God, Maurice, why don't you tell me the truth?

MAURICE. Because I know you, Janet. If you've made up your mind about something you'd refuse to believe me.

JANET. Not if you gave me . . . some proof.

MAURICE. Proof of what?

JANET. Well . . . proof that he didn't come here last night. Proof that you really know nothing about it. And proof that . . .

MAURICE. Yes?

JANET. That Iris isn't going to be accused of . . . of murder . . . if she's innocent.

STELLA. But Janet . . . Iris herself *confessed* that she'd done it.

JANET. I don't *believe* she did it.

STELLA. Don't you believe she intended to?

JANET. Yes. I believe that.

MAURICE. Well then . . . why don't you wait and see what happens? Instead of letting your imagination run amok? Weaving your little theories and hiding things and setting traps? And then falling into them yourself? I don't mind you being ridiculous. I'm used to it. But don't become dangerously so.

(*A pause. He rises and moves away from her.*)

JANET. Am I to mention this?

MAURICE. To whom?

JANET. At the inquest?

(*A pause.* MAURICE *examines the lighter thoughtfully and then puts it back into his pocket.*)

MAURICE. Have you already mentioned it to anyone?

(*A pause.*)

Janet?

JANET. How . . . how could I? I haven't been out.

MAURICE. You were out this morning. You were over at Grey Towers.

STELLA. Brenda only found it this afternoon.

JANET. Yes. Brenda only found it this afternoon.

(*A pause.*)

MAURICE. You won't be asked about it . . . since no one knows. Why should you mention it?

JANET (*rising, in anguish*). Oh my God, Maurice . . . what are we to do?
What about Iris? If it would help her I *must* mention it.
MAURICE. Must?
JANET (*hysterically*). Maurice . . . Maurice . . *did* Colin come here
last night?
MAURICE. No.
JANET. But it isn't true . . . I know it isn't!
MAURICE (*at the top of his voice*). I said, "no"!
JANET (*almost in tears*). It isn't any use, Maurice . . . I know he came
here . . . while Brenda and I were out . . . not only the lighter
. . . there was one of his cigarettes in the . . . the ash tray . . . in
that ash tray there . . . when I came in . . . with Colonel Forbes.
(*She presses her hand to her mouth, shaking her head and beginning
to cry. What she says is almost incoherent.*)
I wish . . . wish I didn't know . . . I didn't try to find out . . .
anything. It's too much . . . responsibility . . . for one person
. . . with poor little Iris at the . . . police station. (*She puts a hand
over her eyes and gropes her way out to the hall.* STELLA *goes quickly
to the door and listens. Then—*)
STELLA. She's gone upstairs.
MAURICE. Well . . . God help us now.
STELLA. But what happened? How did that thing come to be in the garden?
MAURICE. Must have dropped out of his pocket.
(*A pause.*)
STELLA. I suppose she *hasn't* spoken to anyone?
MAURICE. I don't think so. Now listen, Stella. We have to deal with
this. And we have to deal with it quickly.
STELLA. For the moment nobody knows but Janet.
MAURICE. Brenda?
STELLA. She believes it was dropped here yesterday morning.
MAURICE. So there's only Janet. Janet mustn't go out of the house.
And she mustn't use the telephone. My God, the telephone!
(*He goes to the the telephone, picks up the receiver and listens. Then
he replaces it. He now goes quickly to the desk, searches about for a
moment in a drawer and then brings out a small pair of secateurs.*)
STELLA. What are you doing?
MAURICE. I'm going to cut it.
STELLA. Isn't that dangerous?
MAURICE. It's much more dangerous to leave it . . . with the other
telephone upstairs.

(*He draws the curtains, opens the french windows and steps outside. After a moment or two he comes back, closing the french windows again and the curtains.*)

STELLA (*with some agitation*). I don't see how that can help us . . . only until tomorrow! It won't stop Janet saying what she knows at the inquest.

MAURICE. Janet won't go to the inquest. (*He goes to the desk and replaces the secateurs.*)

STELLA (*as before*). How *could* you let that happen? Dropping things! Dropping things! My God!

MAURICE (*angrily*). It was dark! And I had to carry him! And what about you! What about that cigarette in the ash tray! She must have seen it as soon as she came in!

STELLA (*lowering her voice*). Don't let us quarrel. The one thing we have to do now is to keep our heads.

MAURICE. I wonder if she knows anything else.

STELLA. She knows enough. We shall never have another minute of peace as long as she lives.

MAURICE (*softly*). That's exactly what I'm thinking, Stella.

STELLA (*turns to* MAURICE). What do you mean?

MAURICE. I suppose you can guess.

STELLA. You wouldn't . . . you don't . . . (*A moment's pause. Then she bursts out, softly but in terror, seizing the lapels of his coat.*)
Try to keep a hold on yourself, Maurice! Are you going off your head? That's all that's needed to bring the whole of Scotland Yard into it! Even if it looked like an accident . . . even if it *were* an accident . . . who'd ever believe it was? Are you insane?
(*He takes hold of her wrists.*)

MAURICE. Keep calm, Stella. And listen to me. An accident, no. They wouldn't believe it, I agree. But suppose that Janet committed suicide.

STELLA. They wouldn't believe that either.

MAURICE. Wait. Suppose that Janet committed suicide in here . . . tonight . . . while you and I were sitting in the other room . . . with a reliable witness.

STELLA (*softly*). It isn't possible.

MAURICE (*the same*). It's perfectly possible.
She sinks on to the edge of the sofa, staring at him as—

THE CURTAIN FALLS.

SCENE II

There is no change in the appearance of the room. A few hours have elapsed. It is now past nine o'clock of the same evening.
When the curtain rises JANET *is present. She is lying back wearily in the big chair. After a moment there is a knock on the door.* BRENDA *comes in from the kitchen.*

JANET (*apparently with relief*). Oh, it's you, Brenda. (*She sinks into the chair again.*)

BRENDA. Shall I be taking your cup away, ma'am?

JANET. Yes. Yes, do.

(BRENDA *goes to the table on which stands a cup and saucer. There she stops in great disappointment.*)

BRENDA. Oh . . . you haven't touched it!

JANET. I don't want anything, Brenda.

BRENDA. It's a pity. It's a pity. It's at times like this you should keep up your strength. Is there something else you'd care for?

JANET. No . . . nothing.

BRENDA. And what about Mr. Holt? He's had nothing all day either. Shall I take something in to him?

JANET. Where is he, Brenda?

BRENDA. He's in the study, ma'am . . . sitting alone in the study and there's no fire and he has the door open. He'll be dying of cold in there. Shouldn't you go in to him, ma'am?

JANET. I don't think so.

BRENDA. It's so sad to see him grieving there all by himself.

JANET. Don't worry, Brenda. You'd better go upstairs now.

BRENDA. But it's only just on nine o'clock.

JANET (*very much on edge*). Well, do what you like, Brenda . . . will you?

BRENDA. I'll go to my room and if anyone wants anything just let me know.

JANET. Yes, yes. Good night, Brenda.

(BRENDA *goes to the kitchen door. There she turns.*)

BRENDA. It's very queer, Miss Stella going out like that and leaving you both at such a time. Will she be long?

JANET (*struggling to control herself*). I don't know, Brenda. I don't even know where she's gone.

F

BRENDA. It's very sad . . . a family that isn't united when death is in the house. Will she have had anything to eat, ma'am?

JANET. I can't tell you, Brenda! Please go now!

BRENDA (*going*). I wonder should I leave her something. It's all very queer. One doesn't know what to do.

> (*She goes out, closing the door. Left alone, JANET puts her hands to her head and makes a great effort to steady herself: Then she goes to the telephone, picks up the receiver and listens. She rattles the instrument a little with her other hand and then listens again. She is occupied by this when the hall door opens very quietly and MAURICE appears. She has her back to him and does not see him. He watches her for a second or two.*)

MAURICE. Still out of order? (*He speaks very quietly—his voice throughout the whole of the coming scene is gentle—but JANET starts so violently that she drops the receiver with a clatter on to the table.*)

JANET. I . . . I'm sorry . . . I didn't hear you.

MAURICE (*closing the door*). You want to speak to someone?

JANET. I was going to call . . . Joyce. It's strange it being out of order so long . . . so many people must have been trying to get us.

MAURICE. Oh, I don't know.

JANET (*after a pause*). Where has Stella gone to?

MAURICE. I've no idea.

JANET. Is that true?

MAURICE. Do you think I'm telling you a lie?

JANET. Oh, I don't know, Maurice, I don't know what to think about anything.

MAURICE. It's been a day of accusations, hasn't it?

JANET. God knows, I didn't *want* to accuse you.

MAURICE. It's very strange that you should have to do so. But of course circumstantial evidence is invariably confusing. Two or three trivial things—which may have some quite different explanation from the one that you attribute to them—are enough. Once the imagination has begun to work.

JANET (*softly*). I don't see any other explanation. (*In a whisper.*) I only wish I could.

MAURICE. The fact that you can't see another explanation doesn't prove there isn't one. Even in a court of law the prisoner is innocent until he's been proved guilty. And after all you're not a court of law . . . and your emotions are involved. But leaving that aside . . . do you still feel *convinced* . . . really convinced . . that Colin met his death in this house? You've been alone in here for several hours now . . . turning it over in your mind. What conclusion have you come to?

JANET (*shakily*). I . . . I don't *know* what to think . . . I told you. Yes, I've been trying to sort things out. I tell . . . I tell myself it must be so . . . and then I tell myself it *can't* be so and then . . . and now . . . oh God, I wish you'd talk to me, Maurice. (*Her voice trembling.*) I feel so terribly . . . well . . . so, alone.

MAURICE. You're very tired, Janet.

JANET. No, no.

MAURICE (*very gently and kindly*). Oh yes you are. You didn't go to bed at all last night. You haven't eaten anything all day. How can you expect your judgement to be anything but muddled? (*He takes her hands in his, but she withdraws them.*)

JANET. But am I muddled? No.

MAURICE. You said yourself just now . . . you've said it twice since I came into the room . . . you don't know what to think.

JANET. No, no. I've got it all quite clear in my mind. It's just that I'm . . . well, not certain.

MAURICE. Exactly. So first you think one thing and then you're equally convinced of the opposite. Aren't you?

JANET. Well . . . in a way . . . yes.

MAURICE. Well, that's because you're tired. I want you to sleep, Janet. Tomorrow will throw a flood of light on everything. I expect we shall find out lots of things tomorrow . . . things we can't even guess at. (*He takes her hands again. This time she does not withdraw them.*)

JANET. What sort of things?

MAURICE. Janet. Tomorrow morning reason will take a hand in this. And reason will find the guilty and vindicate the innocent . . . of that we can be sure. And it will be based on facts and information . . . not on emotional excitement and ideas. We don't *know* all the facts yet, Janet. I doubt if we know half of them. But tomorrow we shall. In the meantime you must sleep . . . and rest your mind . . . and your imagination, which is playing tricks. I think I'd better put you to sleep and make you rest.

(*A pause.* JANET *does not take her eyes off his.*)

JANET. You mean . . . artificially?

MAURICE. Don't you think it would help you to rest? It always has.

JANET. I think I shall sleep tonight in any case.

MAURICE. I don't think you would, you know.

JANET (*uneasily*). Why not?

MAURICE. I'm afraid you'd simply lie there all night long with your imagination feverishly tying and untying knots.

JANET (*taking her hands away from his*). But I'm very tired, Maurice.

MAURICE. Yes. I can see. Your eyes are tired.

JANET. Why do you want to put me to sleep?

MAURICE. Because you don't know what you're doing or saying, you're so tired.

> (*She puts her hands over her face for a moment. Then she looks at* MAURICE *again*.)

JANET. I'm all right. I don't want you to put me to sleep.

MAURICE. I suggest that you *do* want to sleep, Janet . . . more than anything at this moment.

JANET. Yes, I do want to sleep . . . but I mustn't.

MAURICE. Can you give me a reason why you mustn't sleep?

JANET. No, I . . . I can't. But I feel it.

MAURICE. You can't give me a reason because there isn't one. Is there?

JANET (*staring at him*). I don't know. There was a reason. You muddle me.

MAURICE. It isn't that, my dear. It's simply that there's nothing left except a great desire for sleep. (*He touches her temple gently with his hand. She closes her eyes for a second or two.*) If I put you into a light sleep, Janet, you'll be very rested. It will turn into ordinary slumber. You'll relax. To sleep would do you so much good. You're desperate for sleep. Sleep is all you care about. (*Slowly and softly.*) When I complete the count of five you'll fall into a light and restful sleep. Look at me. One. (*He takes from his pocket a gold pencil and holds it up above her head. She stares at it.*)

JANET (*in a whisper*). Maurice.

MAURICE. You don't want to talk, my dear. You're getting drowsier and drowsier. (*Softly.*) Two (JANET *again closes her eyes for a second or two.*) You can't keep your eyes open, can you? Your eyelids are getting heavier and heavier. You're tired and drowsy and relaxed. You do need sleep. Sleep. (*After a moment.*) Three. (*She closes her eyes. He puts the pencil back into his pocket.*) Your eyes won't keep open any longer. Your arms feel heavy. You are resting placidly. (*Very softly.*) Four. Now you're making no effort at all. You're attending only to my voice. Telling you to sleep. (*In a whisper.*) Five. (*He stands for a second or two looking at her. She remains quite still with her eyes closed.*) Now you're asleep. You have a heavy feeling in your arms. They seem to be weighted down. As heavy as lead. If you try to raise your arms you find you can't. Try to raise your arms. You can't. (JANET *tries. It seems impossible. Quickly.*) You see, you can't! And the more you try the more difficult it is. (*It can be seen that she is struggling to raise her arms but literally cannot.*) All right. Don't try. Relax. Now I'm going to tell you to open your eyes. At present you can't. But when I say, "Open your eyes" you will be able to. But you will continue to sleep. Open your eyes. (JANET *does so. From now on they remain open. But the gaze is a curiously expressionless and unseeing one. It seems to be fixed on something invisible to us, a foot or so in front of her.*) Sit in this chair. (*He puts his hands on the back of the big chair for her and she obeys him. Her movements are extremely slow and the strange, unfocused expression never leaves her face.* MAURICE *goes and puts out some of the lights so that there is just the desk lamp giving a very subdued light. Then he comes back to her. He is much more relaxed now himself. He stands behind her chair, looking down at her.*) Now you're sleeping very lightly, Janet. But you're very glad you let me put you to sleep, aren't you?

JANET (*softly*). Very glad.

MAURICE. And when I put my hands on your head—then you'll go into a far deeper sleep. A very deep sleep indeed. (*He strokes her head for a moment. She sighs, a very deep sigh. Then he goes and sits on the sofa, lying back, quite relaxed. After a moment.*) Now Janet . . . now that you're sleeping very deeply . . . concentrate carefully on what I have to say to you. I'm going to suggest to you that you no longer know what day it is. What day *is* it, Janet? (*She half closes her eyes and makes a quite visible effort to remember.*) You see, you can't remember. And you can't remember what month it is, either. Can you remember what month we are in?

JANET. N—no.

MAURICE. And the year? You can't remember the year either, can you? What year is it?

JANET (*after another effort*). I don't know.

MAURICE. Now I'm going to suggest that you go back in time . . . back into the past. You will feel as though you were back, right back, in the periods I suggest. Now you are back in the time when we were just married. Can you see that?

JANET. Yes.

MAURICE. Can you see yourself and me? Can you see what we are wearing? What we are doing?

(*During the following lines* JANET *seems to burgeon into a state of ecstatic happiness. She begins with a very soft, long-drawn* "Yes".)

JANET. Yes! Of *course.* I'm wearing the yellow dress! The one we bought on our honeymoon in Paris! It *is* a lovely dress! Goodness! What taste you have, to have chosen that! My husband and my yellow dress . . . on the *Boulevard de la Madeleine* . . . on a day in June . . . that was happiness for you! But now we're back in England . . . and you're wearing your black coat and striped trousers which I always say so terrify your patients!

MAURICE. And what are we doing, Janet?

JANET (*contentedly*). Work is over for the day! We have the whole evening to ourselves!

MAURICE. And what are your sensations, Janet?

JANET. Oh God, I'm so happy! I didn't know such happiness existed!

MAURICE. Speak up, Janet. Go on.

JANET (*gloating over her happiness*). You know, Maurice darling, darling Maurice, this is all that anyone could want! To spend the days like this . . . helping you . . . even if it's only in keeping out of the way until you're ready to talk about it all with me . . . that's quite enough! And Stella . . . is she happy? She doesn't resent my intrusion? Does she mind us talking down here . . . sometimes for hours into the night . . . after she's gone up to bed? I don't want to hurt her. I don't want to make the least mistake to spoil it all . . . we mustn't spoil it. And shall we always be so marvellously in love? (*Never looking at him.*) You said last night there was no reason why we shouldn't stay in love like this for good! To think that this has happened to me . . . of *all* people! To me! Janet Taylor! Now Janet Holt! (*Softly.*) Darling, I *do* love you very much!

(MAURICE *cuts in on these last few words rather quickly.*)

MAURICE. Now, Janet, I want you to go back further than that. Please listen carefully. I want you to go back to the day when you first consulted me.

JANET. Yes. (*The air of radiant happiness seems to evaporate. She sits quite still and gradually becomes rigid and hostile.*)

MAURICE. You're going to talk about yourself after all . . . just to see if there's anything in it, aren't you?

JANET. That's what I've come here for today, yes.

(*The hall door opens and* STELLA *appears, wearing her coat.* MAURICE *turns, sees her, rises, turns to* JANET *again and holds out an arm to stop* STELLA *from speaking.*)

MAURICE. Now think about all the things you're going to tell me. (*He half turns his head towards* STELLA *and speaks softly.*) Forbes here?

STELLA. Yes. He's in the study.

MAURICE. What did you tell him?

STELLA. I said you wanted to talk over again what he suggested yesterday.

MAURICE. All right. Now listen. Tell him Janet's very depressed because of what's happened. Say I'm talking to her in here. Say we'll join you in ten minutes or so. When I come in don't leave the room. We must both be with him when it happens. That's all.

(STELLA *goes out.*)

JANET. Was that your wife, Doctor Holt?

(*Throughout these scenes, even when* JANET *speaks directly to* MAURICE, *she never turns her head to look at him. She seems to talk to the air in front of her.*)

MAURICE. No. That was my sister.

JANET (*politely*). She sounds very charming.

MAURICE. But we're here to talk about you, aren't we?

(*During the following lines she seems almost to cave in with wretchedness, becoming small and wizened and injured looking.* MAURICE *takes a revolver from a drawer in the desk and lays it on the blotter, as he sits down.*)

JANET. I'm done for, Doctor Holt . . . finished. (*Very bitterly.*) Oh, I know. I hear what people say. I see the way they look. I see them trying to avoid me. (*With sudden and astonishing anger.*) Yesterday someone who used to be my best friend was coming along the street towards me! I said to myself "Let's see if she'll avoid me!" She evidently saw me in the distance because she suddenly crossed the road and went into a shop! For no reason! (*Suddenly dropping her voice again.*) I don't care though . . . I loathe them all—

MAURICE (*watching her intently*). Go on, Miss Taylor.

JANET. You see, the trouble is, I was never meant to have been born. There was something wrong from the first. My father hated me.

MAURICE. Do you know why?

JANET. Yes, I do know why. He had always wanted a son. When I was little . . . that was before he drank so much . . . he used to go to football matches. I used to wait near the door watching him get ready, hoping he would say "Shall I take you along?" But he used to go . . . without speaking. Later, much later, when he had begun to drink, I didn't dare to go to sleep when he was out. I knew he would be drunk. I knew my mother would get knocked about. I used to go on to the landing and listen. It made me sick.

MAURICE. And what made you feel that this was your fault?

JANET. When he was sent to prison the other girls at school refused to speak to me. I had to be sent to another school. But they found out there, too. I was not allowed in the playground. I had my meals alone. Then I knew that there was something wrong with me. One of the girls once said to me "You'll never live a normal life and you know why". (She puts her face into her hands for a moment.)

MAURICE. And then your mother committed suicide. How old were you?

JANET. Fourteen. After that I knew. I knew that happiness . . . and love . . . were not for me. I knew that whatever I did would be wrong. And in my case it would be wrong even if I did the opposite. I've come to realize that wrong is all I have in me. And when I'm alone I cry and I cry to think that that can never change. (After a moment.) But there is always death. If death is the entrance to a happier world why should I stay in this one where I only suffer? Is suicide an evil thing? Men say so. But men say that of many things that God has given us. And if death is only an eternal, dreamless sleep, what is there to lose? Why not just lie down to sleep?

(She stops. After a moment MAURICE speaks very quietly. She sits quite still, staring in front of her, listening, her face now haggard with misery. While speaking the following lines he loads the revolver.)

MAURICE. Miss Taylor, you have realized many truths. You have courage and I must be frank. Your case appears to me . . . to be quite hopeless. It is true. There are people whose destinies are bad. People who can't be helped.

(She bows her head as though she were being sentenced. He continues, talking low, but driving his phrases home.)

Your mother killed herself. It would be foolish to pretend that you won't do so . . . it's inevitable. I suggest that at this minute . . . if I provided you with the means . . . you would be happy to leave this world where you can never have a place.

JANET (in great anguish). I would . . . oh, I would. (She puts her head down, shakes it from side to side and begins to cry. MAURICE rises and comes round the back of the chair to the other side of her.)

MAURICE. Therefore only good will come of it. There is nothing for you to be afraid of. And it is easy. I will show you.

(*From now on* JANET *focuses on him and on the revolver.*)

Here is a revolver. I suggest to you that . . . in such a case as yours . . . this is the only possible solution.

JANET (*her eyes fixed on it*). I know. It is.

MAURICE. Such an action would be followed by eternal peace.

JANET (*softly*). Yes.

MAURICE. I suggest that *this* is the way to happiness . . . not struggling to live when one was not intended to. If I give this to you . . . you will use it to obtain that happiness.

JANET (*as she continues to stare at it, fascinated*). Oh yes . . . yes.

MAURICE. Then I will give it to you. But you will use it in the way I say.

JANET. Yes, yes.

MAURICE. Now listen very carefully. You will hold it in your hand. I shall go out of the room. You will then count the seconds up to sixty. As you count you will raise the gun to your head. When you have counted up to sixty . . . and on no account before . . . you will press the trigger. I will set it ready for you.

(JANET *looks at it almost greedily while he operates it so that a cartridge is ready for firing. He is close to her and she seizes his left hand and begins to kiss it.*)

JANET. Oh Doctor Holt, thank you . . . thank you . . . thank you for being so kind and so . . . so understanding. (*Greedily.*) Give it to me, give it to me!

MAURICE. Sit up straight. (*She sits up obediently. He puts the revolver into her hand.*) Now you are ready. You will count to sixty. Then you will press the trigger. You will begin to count when I have gone out of the room. I am going out of the room now. (*He goes to the hall door. There he turns and looks at* JANET *again. She remains quite still, facing front.*) I am going now. You will hear me close the door. Then you will begin to count.

(*He goes out and closes the door.* JANET *immediately begins to count, at the rate of about one a second, aloud. As she counts, she raises the revolver to her head so slowly that the movement is almost imperceptible. When she has counted up to about fifteen the light from a torch begins to play up and down the curtains of the french windows and into the room. Then it appears at the little window in the corner up left. Finally* HOWARD *is heard calling and knocking.*)

JANET. Sixteen . . . seventeen . . . eighteen . . . nineteen . . .

HOWARD. Mrs. Holt! Mrs. Holt! (*He apparently comes back to the french windows and shakes them, again calling her name.* JANET *continues to count placidly.*)

JANET. Twenty . . . twenty-one . . . twenty-two . . . twenty-three . . . twenty-four . . . (*So she continues. The door unfortunately opens only from within.* HOWARD *shakes it again, this time very violently, but it holds.*).

Twenty-eight . . . twenty-nine . . . thirty . . . thirty-one . . . thirty-two . . .

(*A pane of glass is shattered.*

JANET *is counting in the forties as* HOWARD *rushes forward and snatches the revolver from her hand. The resulting brainstorm transforms her into a screaming fury.*)

Get away! Get away! Let me go! Give that to me! No! No! No! You mustn't take . . . it . . . no! I want it . . . give it to me! (*She fights like a leopard, scratching, tearing, screaming, struggling desperately to recover the revolver.*)

HOWARD (*at the same time*). No! Don't! Let go! Don't be a fool! Mrs. Holt! Mrs. Holt!

JANET (*in a low groan*). Will you give that back to me! (*At the top of her voice.*) Give it to me! Give it to me! Give it to me! Doctor Holt! Doctor Holt!

(JANET *and* HOWARD *are still fighting and struggling when the hall door bursts open and* MAURICE *rushes in followed by* STELLA *and* COLONEL FORBES. *They stop in amazement.*)

You beast! You have no right! Get out of here! Get out of here, I tell you! Give that back!

HOWARD (*gasping*). Holt! Holt! For God's sake! Speak to her!

(MAURICE *rushes at* JANET *and seizes her. She is crying and groaning,* "No, no".)

MAURICE. All right. All right! Let go! (*He holds her tightly. She is sobbing.*) All right! Calmly now! Calmly! I don't want you to do that! You don't want to do it, either! We've decided you won't do that, after all, Miss Taylor. Quiet now. Be calm.

(*There is a moment of comparative silence.* JANET *hangs in* MAURICE'S *arms.* HOWARD, *whose clothes have nearly been torn off, pushes them back into place.*)

COL. FORBES. My God . . . what happened?

STELLA. Wait! Don't say anything.

MAURICE (*soothingly*). There . . . there . . . it's quite all right . . . you're not to do that after all . . . all right. You don't want to do that any more. (*A moment's pause. She becomes calmer. MAURICE gets her to the sofa.*)

JANET (*exhausted*). I would have done it . . . as you said . . . he stopped me. Doctor Holt! Doctor Holt! Don't leave me!

MAURICE (*softly*). All right, I won't. Be calm now.

(*A moment's pause. JANET seems calmer but completely exhausted. She lies back in the sofa, very dishevelled.*)

HOWARD (*to* FORBES). Colonel Forbes, when I called on you this morning I didn't realize you were going to be invited here tonight to witness a so-called suicide. I only came myself because I rang up Mrs. Holt and found the telephone was disconnected. That made me rather uneasy in view of certain things I'd said to her this afternoon.

COL. FORBES. But, but . . . did she try to kill herself?

HOWARD. She's in a hypnotic trance, Colonel Forbes. (*To* MAURICE.) There's a police car outside, Doctor Holt . . . and you and your sister are under arrest. I must warn you that anything you say . .

MAURICE. All right, all right! I've nothing to say.

HOWARD. Have *you* anything to say, Miss Holt?

STELLA. Simply that whatever applies to my brother applies also to me.

HOWARD (*indicating* JANET). You'd better waken her.

MAURICE (*turning to* JANET). Now, Miss Taylor, we're going to go forward in time . . . into the future. To the day after Colin's death. And all you will remember of this evening . . .

HOWARD. If you don't mind, no amnesia. Her evidence of what occurred tonight may be needed.

MAURICE. No, Mr. Howard. I intend to plead guilty. I don't want her to remember. (*To* JANET.) You will remember nothing about this evening, Janet, nothing at all. Now you are coming back from the past into the present. In a moment I am going to put my hands on your head. When I put my hands on your head you will awaken. Janet, you will face the coming weeks with courage . . . and the coming years with equanimity. You will think less and less about the recent times . . . when evil and misfortune took possession of us . . . and more and more about the better days of long ago . . . the days of the yellow dress and your husband . . . on the *Boulevard de la Madeleine* . . . in June.

He places his hands on her head and bows his own. She closes her eyes and sighs deeply as—

THE CURTAIN FALLS.

PROPERTY PLOT
AND
STAGE PLAN

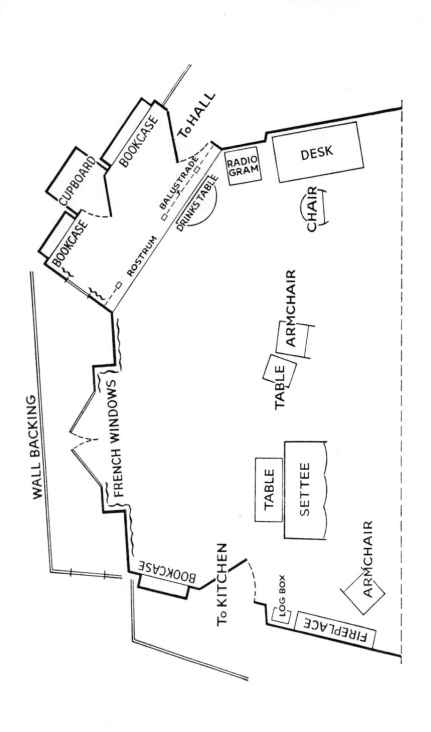